"*Commanding Excellence* highlights three simple proven concepts that are critical to success of a unit in combat or a business in the marketplace. Gary Morton has captured them perfectly. If you want success as a leader in a complex environment read *Commanding Excellence* and follow it!"

—General Bryan "Doug" Brown, US Army, Retired; former commander of US Special Operations Command (SOCOM)

"I've had the good fortune to experience the leadership impact of John Brown firsthand. Without question, Gary captures John's wisdom, clear direction, and unrelenting focus on results. Anyone who wants to understand the fundamentals of successful leadership needs to read this thought-provoking comparison of two inspiring leaders."

—Jim "Coach" Heath, former President, Stryker Instruments

"A compelling read. Based on his personal experience, Gary Morton has analyzed two remarkable organizations and two equally remarkable leaders and served up a timeless story of leadership and how to accomplish that which is seemingly out of reach. If you are a leader or want to be one, this is Leadership 101—and 102."

—General Scott Wallace, US Army, Retired; former commander of US Army Training and Doctrine Command (TRADOC) and, in 2003, V Corps, which comprised the main axis of advance from Kuwait to Baghdad

"Convincing a team to believe in a vision takes sponsorship, commitment, and strong leadership. *Commanding Excellence* demonstrates how to create a culture that everyone commits to from the boardroom to the battlefield. A must-read for anyone who works in a goal-oriented environment."

—Dave Jones, former Sr Vice President for Holiday Inn, created and launched Homewood Suites and Embassy Suites, President and CEO of the Hospitality division for Gaylord Entertainment

"Gary Morton delivers innovative leadership lessons with entertaining insider stories that I wish I had access to when I started Ensighten. If you want to win, read *Commanding Excellence* and see the power of human energy and creativity focused on a common goal."

—Josh Manion, founder and CEO of Ensighten and FIDE chess International Master

"*Commanding Excellence* is a primer on leadership. You'll see how two extraordinary men's personal dedication and drive, coupled with their unquestioned respect for those who worked with and for them, led to a tremendous force multiplier for one tank battalion and a medical manufacturing company. Teamwork is what made it all work, and Gary Morton, who saw it firsthand in both outfits, is the perfect one to tell the story of attained excellence. Read this outstanding story, and see how truly superb outfits can be formed and operate."

—**Lieutenant General Tom Griffin,** US Army, Retired;
former commander of Berlin Brigade and 3rd Armored Division

"Morton witnessed firsthand and has clearly described two examples of extraordinarily effective leadership in two entirely different types of organizations. The author captured specific examples of and portrayed keen insight into effective leaders solving common organizational problems and achieving unique results. The serious student of leadership will complete this entertaining and informative narrative with a handful of practical ideas and would gain even more with repeated study."   —**Major General Richard E. Davis,** US Army, Retired

"Many books have been penned about leadership. *Commanding Excellence* stands out as the best in its approach to define leadership skills and techniques. Morton parallels his experiences as a member of an extraordinary military unit as well as a successful company. His experiences as a team member gave him extraordinary examples of successful leaders. This book is a must-read and highly recommended for those seeking excellence in both personal and team leadership."

—**Lanny R. Copeland,** MD, former President of the American Academy of
Family Physicians and Chief Medical Officer for LifePoint Health

"*Commanding Excellence* reveals the secret sauce to building an organizational passion that wholeheartedly supports those closest to the customer in a business or those on the front lines in a military unit. Such alignment drives astounding success. If you want to deliver exceptional results at any level in an organization, pick up and read this powerful book!"

—**Paul Speigelman,** author of *New York Times* bestseller *Patients Come Second*,
2010 Ernst & Young Entrepreneur of the Year,
founder and CEO of BerylHealth

Inspiring Purpose,
Passion, *and* Ingenuity through
LEADERSHIP THAT MATTERS

COMMANDING

EXCELLENCE

★ ★ ★

GARY MORTON

FOREWORD BY

John W. Brown, former Chairman, President,
and CEO of Strker Corporation, *and*
Colonel Alfred L. Dibella Jr., US Army, Retired;
Former commander of undefeated Task Force 4-68.

GREENLEAF
BOOK GROUP PRESS

This publication is designed to provide accurate and authoritative information in regard to the subject matter covered. It is sold with the understanding that the publisher and author are not engaged in rendering professional services. If expert assistance is required, the services of a competent professional should be sought.

Published by Greenleaf Book Group Press
Austin, Texas
www.gbgpress.com

Distributed by Greenleaf Book Group

For ordering information or special discounts for bulk purchases, please contact Greenleaf Book Group at PO Box 91869, Austin, TX 78709, 512.891.6100.

Design and composition by Greenleaf Book Group
Cover design by Greenleaf Book Group
Cover image: ©iStockphoto.com/OSTILL

Cataloging-in-Publication data is available.

Print ISBN: 978-1-62634-448-8

eBook ISBN: 978-1-62634-449-5

Part of the Tree Neutral® program, which offsets the number of trees consumed in the production and printing of this book by taking proactive steps, such as planting trees in direct proportion to the number of trees used: www.treeneutral.com

TreeNeutral

Printed in the United States of America on acid-free paper

17 18 19 20 21 22   10 9 8 7 6 5 4 3 2 1

First Edition

To John, Fred, and the many extraordinary people of Stryker and Task Force 4-68 who shared these incredible experiences. I am eternally grateful that we had the chance to work or serve together. Though our trials and triumphs, we made a difference in the world; and the show is not over yet.

CONTENTS

FOREWORD

The events described in this book about Task Force 4-68 Armor happened thirty years ago, but like the 1980 Miracle on Ice in Olympic lore, 4-68's annihilation of the vaunted and invincible Opposing Forces (OPFOR) in 1986 at the Army's National Training Center endures in Army annals. It was never done before. It has never been done since.

When I look back on those magical, almost mythical days, I obviously do so through my own personal memory reticle—as does Gary Morton and every other man who served in that special combat unit. But what Gary does so beautifully in this book is combine all our reticles into one giant aperture, then analyze the reminiscences, and, finally, distill them down into a handful of precious categories. No one else I know has both the boots-on-the-ground expertise and the intellectual and literary skills to do that. Then he does the same thing with John Brown's Stryker, which I have come to learn was an astoundingly successful medical-device manufacturer with a superb leader whose accomplishments Gary also hugely influenced.

I think that what may be most fascinating to students of leadership or management—be they military or civilian—is Gary's documentation and analysis of the identical factors that enabled the uncommon success of both organizations. Funny, though, the more I think about it, I suppose the operational similarities between a medical-device manufacturer and an army combat task force should not have surprised me so much; after all, we both operated on the extremity of the life-and-death spectrum, albeit opposite ends.

But make no mistake: This book captures the essence of two *results-oriented* odysseys. It is therefore most useful for those who can establish a crystal clear, meaningful, uncompromising objective and then generate the unbridled passion and commitment to pursue and achieve it. It recognizes the preeminent value of people along the journey, but it doesn't pander to them en route. No "participation trophies" on this voyage. No social engineering, and no political correctness. It's about everyone signing up and then pulling their weight, so the whole becomes greater than the sum of its parts. That's the true test or the very essence of leadership and management anyway, right?

Finally, please permit me this opportunity to relay a brief message to all those over the years who have so kindly inquired as to why I left the Army I fervently loved after only twenty-one years and forsook the promotions they so charitably predicted. There were two reasons:

Task-force-level command is the final occasion for a senior combat officer to enjoy personal, frequent interaction with his "Killer Angels"—the soldiers he loves and leads. It's the last opportunity to teach, motivate, and ultimately exclaim, "Follow me!" Personally, I could never replace that exhilarating daily fulfillment and privilege, even with thrones or symphonies or triumphal arches.

Two years after departing TF 4-68 Armor, I was selected for full colonel and an overseas brigade command in Germany. Coincidently, it was also the same time my only son was just beginning his four-year curriculum at a US service academy—a demanding educational choice for which I personally lobbied. Knowing full well the extreme commitment it would require, I was not prepared to deprive him of the vital support his loving parents could provide by remaining in close proximity. He turned out great, and I like to think that staying nearby made a difference.

I am humbled and honored to be mentioned in this book, particularly since there were so many heroes in my midst. Many are mentioned herein, like Moore, Carruthers, Morton, Roacha, Piskel, Campbell, and Styles. But there were also many others like Gillman, my loyal and dedicated executive officer, and Arruda, my command sergeant major. There were so very, very many, and all of them deserve equal acclaim. They have my everlasting gratitude, admiration, and love.

—Alfred L. Dibella Jr.

I have read two extraordinary books about Stryker. The first, Jim Collins's *Great by Choice* presented an outsider's view based on reading every shred of paper ever written about the company. The second, *Commanding Excellence*, which you are holding in your hands, accurately portrays an insider's view from someone who knows all the agony, pain, and triumph from living through the gyrations of a Stryker experience. It intimately relates how to be competitive and how to win.

Gary Morton was a leader of one of Stryker Corporation's most successful initiatives. His book contains two fascinating stories written by a single author. One story is about his experience as a young lieutenant in an intensive military training program, and the other is about his later experience within Stryker. Both narratives are captivating, and for those individuals interested in learning about leadership, much can be gained in reading these accounts.

—John W. Brown

Introduction

TWO EXTRAORDINARY

ORGANIZATIONS

L ate in the Cold War era, Task Force Fourth Battalion, Sixty-Eighth (4-68) Armor, out of Fort Carson, Colorado, accomplished what top military officials from the United States and NATO thought impossible. During that era, the most realistic and demanding battle simulation exercises entailed rotating through a series of engagements at the National Training Center (NTC). On some of the planet's most desolate ground—Fort Irwin, in California's Mojave Desert—the maneuver units endured a highly intensive month of evaluation and training. Using state-of-the-art laser-engagement and computer-tracking systems, they would fight an Opposing Force (OPFOR) trained in the tactics and doctrine of the Soviet Army.

Combined arms task forces would generally fight nine force-on-force battles. The OPFOR knew the terrain: they greatly outnumbered the US forces (reflecting the USSR's numerical advantages); they were very well trained; and they had excellent morale. A typical US unit would win one or two of the nine battles; a rare team with luck on their side might win four. Once in a decade, a phenomenal task force would have a positive record and win five of the nine. Task Force 4-68 Armor did the impossible, achieving a 9–0 record in the spring of 1986. No other unit has ever won every battle against the OPFOR.

4-68's success was such an anomaly that senior generals and leaders at every level took notice and sought to understand the secrets to our success. The approach and basic tactics of 4-68's NTC rotation served to refine US maneuver doctrine. They became part of the operational concepts used by the forces under General Norman Schwarzkopf in Desert Storm and, later, in the second Iraq conflict.

Leading 4-68 to this unprecedented success was an inspirational young Lieutenant Colonel named Alfred L. Dibella Jr. Just twelve months into his command, Dibella turned the least combat-worthy unit in the Fourth Mechanized Infantry Division, of which 4-68 Armor was a part, into the most lethal, most effective, and most combat-ready unit in the US Army. What 4-68 achieved is akin to a last-place collegiate football team hiring a new head coach and becoming national champion in a single year, dominating every game on their way to the title.

In a completely different field, Stryker, a medical-device manufacturer, also delivered unprecedented results. From humble beginnings, Stryker grew its earnings by more than 20 percent every year and every quarter of every year for twenty-eight years. This streak was interrupted only once, when it acquired a company about its own size. Twelve months following this acquisition, Stryker was right back on track, delivering a compounded 20 percent over the preacquisition results. Stryker's consistent growth facilitated stock market returns that outperformed icons such as Microsoft or Berkshire Hathaway over the long term.

One senior leader during this growth period told and retold a famous story about a fellow sales rep who, in 1979, had received a bonus of $5,000 for his excellent results. He was debating what to do with the money—install a swimming pool at his home or invest in Stryker at the IPO? He decided to install the swimming pool. By 2004, the rep could only look upon the pool and lament that at $3.25 million, it was the most expensive backyard pool in the country. Few, if any, publicly traded stocks during any twenty-five-year period have equaled those returns. The company grew from less than $20M in annual sales of stretchers, cast cutters, and wedge-turning frames into a $4 billion medical-device powerhouse, with products from orthopedic implants to surgical instruments, endoscopic equipment, hospital beds, and EMS ambulance stretchers.

Like 4-68 Armor, Stryker was blessed to have a truly exceptional leader during this unprecedented growth period. John W. Brown presided as the chairman, president, and CEO as Stryker evolved into one of the most respected and successful companies on the planet. When Brown joined the company, it was a small boutique firm with a couple of innovative products built off expiring patents. The transformation into a medical-device behemoth more than 25,000 percent larger over his twenty-eight years of leadership was remarkable.

I had the good fortune to be inside both of these organizations during these extraordinary periods—as a lieutenant in 4-68 and as a vice president in Stryker. My most lasting memory is the remarkable similarity between their intense internal environments. These were two very different organizations—a military unit and a capitalist enterprise—yet the crazed obsession for excellence within them was nearly the same. In this book, I will describe how the top leader's pervasive influence captured the hearts and minds of those inside and created an ethos of inevitable excellence, out of which came unprecedented success.

THREE MAGICAL THEMES

Although each leader's style and personality were quite different, the similar influence they wielded drove the unstoppable trains. This was the secret sauce. In attempting to describe its unique ingredients in early drafts, I worked to fit the experiences into known leadership or management theories; but the descriptions always fell short. These were very special organizations with exceptional leaders whose stories demanded a groundbreaking narrative. After numerous conversations with people from both organizations and deep reflection with the two leaders, simplicity emerged as key to the story, with three common themes capturing the essence:

1. Absolute clarity of purpose
2. Empowered obsession
3. Unleashed creativity

Capitalizing on these interconnected themes, Fred Dibella and John Brown invisibly orchestrated thousands of individual actions into a cohesive masterpiece resulting in the stunning successes of their organizations.

ABSOLUTE CLARITY OF PURPOSE

Dibella rallied his soldiers to embrace the goal from a stage—an announcement that made the goal concrete by calling it out in public. Every training exercise, every After-Action Review, every physical training run, essentially every significant activity was tied to the goal of gaining the combat proficiency necessary to go 9–0 at the National Training Center. All distractions were eliminated or deliberately deemphasized. With similar effect, Brown resolutely made 20-percent growth the pervasive objective of the business—every month, every quarter, every year. Bonuses, performance reviews, and monthly, quarterly, and annual reviews were all tied to the goal. It became an imprinted behavior: No division leader would consider a plan that delivered less than 20-percent earnings growth.

The purpose defined what we would do and what we would not do, what was important and what was trivial. Everyone throughout the organization—from the company commander to the private serving in the mess hall and from the corporate vice presidents to the receptionist—knew the goal, acknowledged how important it was to the organization, and understood how they could contribute to its achievement.

EMPOWERED OBSESSION

Most respected leaders work determinedly toward accomplishing key objectives and demonstrate serious effort in the process. Dibella and Brown did this at an entirely different level. Their efforts toward achieving the organization's purpose were maniacal. They displayed an obsession that few could ever attempt to match. But it was not only their personal fervor that led to such extraordinary results; it was their ability to spread a similar passion throughout their organizations. By empowering individuals and entrusting them with authority and autonomy, they spread the obsession into every level. For the many captivated by the process, we felt deep personal ownership of the goal and knew that our actions were absolutely essential to attaining it.

Dibella emphasized his goal of beating the OPFOR at every meeting and every battalion-level event, and he made it clear that he walked the talk and talked the walk. Unlike many career-protecting field-grade officers, he challenged Army doctrine, took personal risks in training, and put his own reputation on the line, setting the example by excelling in the same qualifications that every soldier and tank commander had to meet. Such fanatical determination infected the unit.

Before one crucial defensive battle, my commander, Dave Carruthers, awoke in the middle of the night in a cold sweat. He gathered all of the lieutenants to scout a route for our tanks in case the OPFOR came down one of the potential approaches into the battalion's position. Obsessed with winning, Carruthers could not sleep for fear that if the enemy used this approach, they could bypass the majority of Alpha Company. It was about 2:00 a.m. on a cold desert morning when we returned to our bunks.

Whereas Dibella boldly announced his goal from a stage, Brown communicated the importance of Stryker's goal in a more subtle but no less forceful manner. For example, in an internal letter he wrote: "Twenty percent is the water level. Above 20 percent, you can breathe and see the world; it is good. Below 20 percent, you are underwater, suffocating, drowning; it is horrible."

This led one of the fiery divisional leaders to create the Snorkel Award, which was given to the president of the division exhibiting the slowest growth in the previous period. In the environment at the time, no one questioned whether such an award should exist. Every leader was accountable. In a warped way, the humor implicit in the award helped in the acceptance process and was quickly translated into extraordinary effort to get the snorkel moved on to a different division.

Brown displayed his obsession most notably through his work ethic. In the dark winter evenings after business trips, as I walked through the airport parking lot to my frozen car, the Stryker corporate office building was visible in the distance. It was common to see only one light in the building: Mr. Brown toiling away in the top corner office on some important business. No one worked harder than the CEO, but following his example, many acquired a similar commitment to the goal.

UNLEASHED CREATIVITY

These leaders deeply internalized the difficulty of achieving the purpose and knew that effective ingenuity and powerful new ideas were essential. They created cultures in which innovation mattered, and innovation that mattered flourished. It was perhaps in this area that each leader would become the most personally involved. Regardless of what stood in our path, we would find a way around.

Their fundamental passion for creativity stemmed from the obsession with achieving the purpose. This is a key point important for any organization: Innovation for its own sake is not necessarily useful, but innovation that matters—that is aligned with the overall purpose of the organization—drives success. With a clear goal, an inspired team bestowed with unbounded creative latitude will work wonders.

Dibella discarded the notion of rank or a chain of command when it came to brainstorming new ideas. He embraced every new concept that could move us closer to the goal. He instilled the belief throughout the organization that going 9–0 would require not only executing well against OPFOR but also using radically different methods. He innately understood that creativity is a different talent from those that might foster a successful Army career. We would have to capitalize on the ingenuity of soldiers at every level, not just commanders or senior officers. In that spirit, After-Action Reviews included company commanders and brand-new second lieutenants; anyone could have the floor. With this frame of mind, the battalion developed an innovative approach that profoundly affected US Army small-unit doctrine in the years to come.

For his part, Brown was masterful at inspiring effective creativity within the Stryker divisions. He set up the company's organizational structure to foster innovation. Autonomous divisions competed to have the best growth numbers, and those with successful new products were likely to be on top. Remember that the obsession, however, was not just growth but 20-percent growth every quarter. One-hit wonders were praised when they hit, but they could just as easily be scolded the following year for failing to grow off their home-run year. Stryker required innovation that endured, seeds that would sprout into thriving, constantly growing trees, and eventually lush, ever-expanding forests.

Brown also celebrated successful new ideas throughout the company. In a monthly letter, he would sing the praises of the marketing and product-development teams that launched winning new products, sales teams that exploited innovative approaches to selling and distributing the products, and manufacturing teams that improved results with new tools and techniques. He took a keen interest in the technological progress of every division.

Explaining his simple philosophy of growth at one meeting, Brown remarked, "If we continue to provide the best products and have the best sales teams in our respective markets, then success will be likely to follow."

Being the best necessitated unleashing creativity and focusing innovation at all of the company's divisions.

FOCUSED SIMPLICITY

These three metathemes—absolute clarity of purpose, empowered obsession, and unleashed creativity—were the secret sauce that allowed these organizations to achieve results in the top 1 percent of the top 1 percent. But there was nothing complicated about creating the sauce. John Brown at Stryker and Fred Dibella in Task Force 4-68 Armor defined a crystal clear organizational goal in simple, measurable terms. They maintained a monomaniacal commitment to achieve the goal and spread that commitment to everyone. And they harnessed every ounce of creative energy toward achieving the goal. Purpose, passion, and ingenuity drove everything. In the end, these organizations achieved the impossible. So can you.

PART 1

ABSOLUTE CLARITY OF PURPOSE

Perhaps the most important question for the leader of any organization is *What are we trying to achieve?* John Brown and Fred Dibella's unequivocal clarity in defining an overriding purpose answered this question in simple, powerful terms that left no room for misunderstanding. In doing so, they greatly streamlined decision processes throughout their organizations. Every leader, manager, and team member knew the top leader's most important priority. In most cases, decisions did not require higher-level endorsement; the purpose served as a guide.

Excellent ideas abound about crafting a mission statement, communicating it, and its overall importance. The process of developing the mission can galvanize a team. If done well, the statement helps to define and clarify priorities and timeless principles for the organization. With all due respect to such efforts, however, the clarity within Task Force 4-68 Armor and Stryker was something beyond a well-crafted mission statement or even a mission statement on steroids.

The absolute clarity of purpose pervaded every activity. It was in the backdrop of countless decisions large and small that were made every day and at all levels inside those organizations. Through these thousands of individual decisions, an invisible hand moved every activity toward the same goal. You knew you were right if you decided on a course of action that would help us win battles at the NTC, or grow by 20 percent. The collective results were magical.

By themselves, the three-word statements of the purpose at Stryker or TF 4-68 did not sound particularly inspirational. Neither appealed to the human capacity to promote the greater good, advance the state of the art in a field, or improve human lives. Yet such simple focus enabled those types of noble achievements to occur. Each organization made significant positive contributions in their areas of endeavor and in the lives of their members. Clearly defining success ripped away the hubris of overcomplicated declarations of priorities and allowed people to do what they did best every day. The people then achieved those noble goals.

These simple, highly visible measurements also promoted a feeling of solidarity that left little room for excuses or political "spin." Results were what mattered. Everyone and every team knew where they stood, and each leader constantly emphasized progress toward achieving the three-word purpose. Every group encounter, every meeting, every breakfast, every luncheon, and every awards ceremony was a chance to define progress. Whether it was an After-Action Review, a presentation at a divisional sales meeting, or a perfect-attendance lunch with manufacturing teams, Brown and Dibella drove it home.

They also structured their organizations to bring critical resources to bear at the precise moments when decisive actions would directly affect achieving the purpose. For Dibella this meant lining up behind the soldiers and commanders on the front line. Those closest to the battle knew best what was happening. Commanders on the front were empowered to make the key decisions and call the shots during an operation. It was utterly clear that the battalion staff, the support units, and the service support units were to ensure that those in direct contact with the enemy would have every conceivable resource available to win.

Similarly, John Brown organized Stryker to line up behind the sales teams that were fighting to win each individual sale. As Stryker became involved in different markets with distinct customers in each, this meant a fiercely decentralized structure. Each customer-focused division unleashed the intensely competitive strength of self-directed teams and the collaborative power of a focused organization marching in lockstep to achieve a common purpose. Formal and informal chains of command were all oriented to drive responsibility and accountability to those on the front.

Dibella and Brown further structured their teams and chose roles for the organization's leaders with an extreme bias toward the strengths of individual leaders and managers. This was an element of the clarity of purpose. Dibella developed Task Force 4-68's company missions around the perceived strengths of each of the commanders, their company's respective sergeants, and soldiers. At Stryker, respect for each individual's unique capabilities was always part of the culture under Brown. As the company's relationship with the Gallup organization deepened in the 1990s and early 2000s, Stryker became a mecca for strengths-based management and selection. Gallup provided a vocabulary for these strengths and statistically validated methods to help identify, quantify, and exploit them.

Finally, each of these leaders had excellent support from higher-level leadership with regard to the purpose. Fort Carson's commanding general's view of the mission of each maneuver battalion was highly congruent with Lieutenant Colonel (LTC) Dibella's efforts to win at NTC.

Stryker's Board of Directors consistently demonstrated an unwavering endorsement of John Brown's goals and the 20-percent growth objective. The higher levels did not interfere; rather they facilitated, encouraged, and worked to provide essential resources. Three notable elements of this higher-level support were common between 4-68 and Stryker:

1. The higher-level leadership steadfastly endorsed the purpose and demonstrated this endorsement through their actions.
2. Dibella and Brown could effectively leverage this higher-level support and could receive backing for all reasonable requests for actions to support achieving the purpose.
3. Perhaps most important, the higher-level leadership gave Brown and Dibella nearly complete freedom to run their own ships.

1

CLARITY OF PURPOSE

IN 4-68 ARMOR

Following an intense field-training exercise a few months after he assumed command, Dibella planned a galvanizing event. He brought every soldier of the task force and closely related support units into the main auditorium at Fort Carson. He began his presentation by detailing the many challenges that units face in confronting the OPFOR at the National Training Center.

The delivery was brutally honest. The OPFOR literally picked most units apart. They had nearly every advantage: numerical superiority, specially selected leaders, intimate knowledge of the terrain, exceptional maintenance organizations, high morale, and extraordinarily experienced troops. They seemed unbeatable.

Then Dibella expounded on what he believed would be their weaknesses: They followed Soviet doctrine to a tee, which made them predictable. Their equipment, while well maintained, was technologically inferior. They had no thermal-imaging sights, only infrared. Their tanks carried less ammunition. Their air and artillery support was slower to react and less deadly than ours. They were used to winning and could be overconfident.

He issued the challenge that was to become our all-pervasive purpose over the next nine months, "Most units are lucky to win a battle or two. A great battalion wins four or five of the battles."

He let those facts settle with the crowd, then, with a deliberate southern Illinois accent, he exclaimed: "Ain't *nobody* ever been *nine and oh*! That is what we are going to do!"

That became the rally cry and the goal. It was simple, measurable, and meaningful, and every soldier would make a difference in achieving it. It was bold, inspired competitive juices, and was just beyond what seemed possible.

CLARITY AND FOCUS

I was sitting in front of two hardened and skeptical master sergeants from the brigade maintenance support unit. They had heard similar rally cries from other battalion commanders whose units went out to Fort Irwin and were summarily humiliated.

"Here we go again," they lamented. "Everybody thinks rah-rah will beat the OPFOR, then they go out there and get their asses kicked."

What made 4-68 Armor different? Why did that task force prove the master sergeants wrong? Well, first of all, this wasn't just a cheer to energize the team; Dibella *meant* it. He would do everything and anything to support the ideas, processes, commanders, and soldiers to do whatever was necessary (and ethical) to go 9–0. He ensured that his staff and all of his commanders were totally focused in the same fashion.

For example, some battalions spent weeks preparing for a parade in front of the new assistant division commander. At 4-68, we did not have time for lengthy parade preparation; we spent only a day. Being great at close-order parade drill was not going to help us win at the NTC. We spent our time refining our battle plans and drilling the requirements and expectations into every soldier.

I cannot emphasize this point too much. Most leaders define aggressive goals for their organizations. Most leaders work diligently and drive their organizations to achieve the goals. Only a few deliver truly extraordinary results. The crucial difference lies in the distinction between simple high expectations and an all-embracing goal whose achievement becomes pervasive in the organization. The absolute clarity of purpose Dibella delivered served as an umbrella over the priorities of the battalion. It forced us to face with brutal and complete honesty any problems or issues that would impede its achievement.

Apple CEO Tim Cook, and Steve Jobs before him, follows a similar ethos at Apple. When discussing the keys to success, Jobs remarked multiple times, "Deciding what not to do is as important as deciding what to do."

Such focus cuts like a finely sharpened sword through the hubris of corporate bureaucracy. For 4-68 Armor, it was a guiding light.

Truly deciding what not to do has a profound impact on the organization. Many leaders struggle with the *truly* part of that sentence. They will say that the priorities are A, B, and C, but when outside scrutiny concentrates on priority D, they waver. Most, with all the best intentions, attempt to achieve every potential goal. They want to go 9–0 and win the parade. Deciding what not to do clarifies the purpose.

SIMPLICITY

Dibella also had a driving passion to keep things simple. The most cogent element of this was the adoption of the singular purpose. We were not just going to win a battle or two; we were going to defeat OPFOR *every time*. It was audacious, measurable, inspiring, and straightforward. During his presentation, Dibella laid out an uncomplicated plan that had meaning for everyone. In describing the kinks in the seemingly impenetrable armor of the OPFOR, he also described an innovative methodology we were developing to provide an outline for every line soldier's responsibility in every type of operation. He described some critical observations from NTC veterans regarding the intelligence-gathering methods of the OPFOR and how we would use their methods against them. He described the shortcomings in Soviet maneuver doctrine, how the OPFOR would religiously follow the doctrine, and how we could use our knowledge of it to defeat them.

THE *SILVER LIONS PLAYBOOK*

Dibella described how the battalion's leadership was wrapping up all of these thoughts into a tangible definition of how we were going to fight our battles, which he aptly named the *Silver Lions Playbook*.

He described the genesis and reasons for the playbook, starting with a story about Jim Young, who had taken over the Army (West Point) football-coaching job in 1983. Young moved into a program with a storied past that had been struggling in the 1970s and early 1980s. The experienced coach observed several key characteristics of the Army team: They were undermanned in the sense that their players were smaller and slower than those of their opponents. The players were stressed for time, with an uncompromising full academic load along with cadet duties. Having an entire team with mandatory enrollment in demanding courses such as electrical engineering could distract considerably from the football program. However, he also observed that, man for man, these players showed uncommon discipline, and they exhibited great cohesion as a team. The challenges they endured in academy life could become a source of team strength. They were quick learners and could execute simple plays together with precision. Young believed he could fuse them into a high-performance organization.

Dibella also recounted Young's challenge in deciding what kind of offensive program he could create to overcome these weaknesses and capitalize on these strengths. The experienced coach determined that a *wishbone* offense might work. For those unfamiliar with football, the wishbone is an offensive methodology based on a formation having three backs in the backfield, making the formation shaped like a wishbone when viewed from above. Its landmark play is the triple option, where the quarterback has the options of handing off to the full back, who will run off the guard; keeping the ball and running off tackle himself; or pitching the ball to an outside back if the defense crashes the line. It is considered the consummate team offense. It is a simple, run-heavy methodology. There are essentially only six offensive plays to master: three to the right and three to the left.

The wishbone methodology would compensate for the weaknesses of the Army team: Size was less critical than strength. Speed was less critical than quickness. The flashiness of other NCAA Division I-A players could be overcome with toughness and the martial art–like capability of being able to use your opponent's momentum and your own to your advantage. It compensated for the players' lack of time because it was simple to implement. Young wanted to ensure the practice time was spent developing excellence in executing each individual's task in a limited number of plays. The team would drill their six plays until they could execute with great precision. The handoff smoothly placed, the pitch perfectly timed, the blocking assignments down cold.

The wishbone also relied on great discipline and unit cohesion. It counted on eleven men on the field all understanding what was happening with the offense, every player reading their block, every player executing their assignment. No one person was out for themselves or attending to their individual statistics. The quarterback would likely get hit on every play, but that would not matter; it was about the number of yards gained. The Army team began to act and react like a single unit. This simplicity lent itself to the discipline and unit cohesion they already had. Positive results in the games quickly followed.

By his second year, Young had dramatically turned the program around. The team's record went to 8–3–1. They won the highly competitive games against their service academy rivals at Air Force and Navy and capped off the season by beating the Michigan State Spartans at the Peach Bowl. It was the best season Army had seen in nearly two decades.

Dibella (a former quarterback himself) was inspired by the turn-around in Army football. He described how the situation Jim Young faced when he first walked onto the field at West Point was fundamentally similar to that of our combined arms task force at Fort Carson.

We were undermanned in the sense that the OPFOR outnumbered our forces and had their pick of soldiers. OPFOR was nearly always at full strength, whereas the units at Fort Carson needed to beg and borrow personnel just to fill out their authorized positions. Even with every position filled, Task Force 4-68 Armor would go to the NTC as a 2–2 task force, composed of two mechanized infantry companies (about 110 soldiers each) and two tank companies (14 tanks each), with a total of 40 tank-killing systems. The OPFOR regiment had 140 tank-killing systems and an all-in strength of over 2,000 soldiers.

We had constrained time to practice along with significant additional responsibilities. It would be important to maximize the use of available field training by keeping the concept of our operations simple and the responsibilities of every person on the team absolutely clear. That way, the soldiers could drill the actions that they were most likely to execute in the battles. The playbook became our implementation of a simplified offense for maneuver operations, like the wishbone. It brought focus to our field training. Similar to most Army units at the time, we were a unit filled with soldiers who had volunteered. They came with a great capacity for discipline and potential for unit cohesion, but the constant personnel shuffle and myriad responsibilities outside of combat readiness handicapped our preparedness. The playbook helped to concentrate our available training time on the missions and sub-missions each individual unit would perform in a play. It was a way to capitalize on the strengths of our soldiers, NCOs, and officers.

The idea of simplifying our operations into a set of clearly defined plays was an act of genius. Instead of devising a completely new maneuver plan for each mission, it systemized our concept of the operation with straightforward methodologies for moving, attacking, and defending. In doing so, the playbook served as a quintessential instrument of clarity down to the individual soldier level. By grasping the basic ideas in the playbook, the purpose—going 9–0 against the OPFOR—became ever more meaningful. Every unit and every soldier could understand their role and concentrate their training on their assignment. We practiced and practiced until each company, platoon, and tank crew could execute with precision. In the background, the soldiers also gained a heightened awareness that their actions made a difference. What they were doing fit into the simple concept of a well-designed battle play that was easily understood.

During the auditorium presentation, the playbook was in its infancy. Dibella, his staff, and the commanders had many general ideas, but it would take several months to flesh out the plan for each of the plays and many more to drill them to precision. The process of building the playbook and then drilling it to near perfection would further serve to empower a shared obsession for winning and unleash transformational creativity in the unit.

Winning every battle at that phenomenal training center would require radical new approaches in how we conducted combat operations. The playbook became a vital part of that process. In a unit without such clear focus, the playbook could easily have lost momentum, fallen into disuse, or become a pet project of just a few. Even for units with a more immediate war-fighting mission on the border with the Eastern Bloc, the passion for combat proficiency was not as extreme as that in 4-68.

One of the former captains in the task force recalled a subsequent assignment on the border, "You would think that our focus on war-fighting skills would be absolutely crystal clear, but just the opposite was true because we had a commander who let all these little ankle-biter things be more important than improving those skills."

Beating the OPFOR would require exceptional command and

control of the engagement. If we could develop a solid set of operational concepts, capture them in the plays, and get all of the soldiers to know their roles, it could give us a major leg up. The playbook boiled down the complicated process of task-force-level combat operations into simple steps that every soldier could understand.

We developed six plays: two offensive or deliberate attack plays, defensive plays for narrow and wide fronts, and two movement or movement-to-contact plays. In learning the plays, every frontline soldier knew their assigned role and the overall maneuver. It made acting and reacting swifter and more decisive. It integrated every combat support and combat service support system.

On a deliberate attack into an objective, for example, the play allowed everyone to understand who would be supporting them on their right, left, rear, or front. The fire-support unit could grasp the general flow of each battle and could develop a sense of which missions should take priority. The Air Defense Artillery (ADA) unit could understand where they should expect the friendly maneuver units to be during various types of operations and could develop their own "plays" for effective ADA deployment. The helicopter and fixed-wing air support could anticipate where the friendly and enemy units would be on the battlefield. We practiced it, we drilled it, and we refined it. We worked tirelessly until the unit could execute the plays flawlessly and individual soldiers had mastered their parts, as Dibella would say, "down to a gnat's ass."

Thirty years after the rotation, Mark Pires, a former captain in the task-force operations staff, recalled the atmosphere. "As we developed that thing [the playbook], not only was it a great collaborative effort from everybody involved, but everybody understood their role as part of the bigger picture, and everybody understood what those around them were doing. Everyone understood their piece, why their role was important, and how they meshed with everybody else."

This utterly pervasive and absolute clarity of purpose conferred a sense of togetherness and teamwork. The playbook codified it for our battles. Our six plays provided a widely understood framework for decisions large and small that were made every second by soldiers at all levels. Through thousands of individual decisions, an invisible hand moved every activity toward the same pervasive goal. The collective result was magical.

2

CLARITY OF

PURPOSE IN ACTION

AT THE NTC

I must admit that, after the auditorium presentation, there were still many skeptics. In particular, the NTC veterans who had experienced firsthand the unmatched combat skill of the hardened OPFOR troops thought it was a bit far-fetched that any unit could beat them in every battle. These veterans wanted to buy in to the purpose, but in the back of their minds they couldn't help feeling it was a bridge too far. Their fallback was to put the same energies into doing everything humanly possible to improve combat effectiveness, essentially the same things you would do if going wholeheartedly after the 9–0 goal.

Fellow platoon leader Bobby Campbell had been to the NTC in an advisor role to assist in training a National Guard battalion. "What I saw when I was at the NTC earlier," he said, "was that there's no way to beat these guys. I don't know that I personally ever believed we could go 9–0, but I knew we could give the OPFOR one hell of a fight."

After the first wins against the OPFOR, the momentum built. Campbell recalled, "We all started to believe it as we went further into the rotation."

When we started winning in training exercises leading up to the NTC, many began to believe. When we started winning battle after battle during the actual NTC rotation, even the veterans began to feel that it might be possible. Toward the end, 9–0 was our universal battle cry, and for the many months leading up to the rotation, it made our priorities crystal clear.

SIMULATING MODERN WARFARE

The National Training Center (NTC) was a phenomenal facility. A rotation provided the ultimate test of a unit's combat capability during a grueling, month-long exercise in the heat and blowing sand of the Mojave Desert. US-based task-force-level commanders would have one chance to take their unit to the NTC and face the formidable OPFOR. Soldiers would travel to the desert with just their basic equipment and would borrow all of their heavy equipment (tanks, armored personnel carriers, trucks, jeeps, self-propelled artillery, etc.) from the stores at Fort Irwin. With two days to prepare at the desert motor pool, every one of the major pieces of equipment and every soldier would also install the Multiple Integrated Laser Engagement System (MILES) hardware to make the combat simulation as realistic as possible. The MILES's sophistication and the overall environment at NTC represented the closest thing to actual warfare that modern armies had ever seen.

We outfitted the vehicles with a belt of laser sensors. Tank crews inserted a laser transmitter in the main gun tube and connected it to the tank's firing system, along with a Hoffman device that would set off a small explosive charge to simulate the main gun firing. The laser could only fire as fast as a crew could realistically load the main gun. All vehicles installed a large external "kill" light, which indicated a hit or miss. We outfitted machine guns and rifles with transmitters that shot lasers when soldiers fired blank rounds. Dismounted soldiers donned a harness with sensors, as well as a halo of sensors on their helmets. Each laser transmitter mimicked the effective range of the weapon to which it was slaved.

When a laser hit a sensor, it carried information about the shooter's weapon and ammunition. The target's MILES system then calculated a random number roll and consulted a casualty probability lookup table to determine the outcome. For example, a frontal hit by an armor-piercing round from an M60A3 tank striking a simulated Soviet T-62 from long range might only record the shot as a near miss. This would cause the T-62's kill light to blink rapidly a few times, send a near miss beep through that crew's internal intercom, and temporarily incapacitate the tank's MILES system. A hit on the side of a tank by a main gun would likely result in a kill; the kill light would blink continuously and buzz through the tank's intercom. A MILES transmitter emulating an M16 rifle could not harm an Armored Personnel Carrier (APC), but it could still "kill" a commander visible in the hatch of the vehicle.

At NTC, most of the MILES systems were coupled with a real-time data link that transmitted position and event data back to a central site for collection and display. The central site collected statistics on each tank and major weapon system's kill-versus-killed record and a host of other information. During After-Action Reviews, the Observer–Controllers could literally replay the battle on a giant computer screen and review key events. For units in the Cold War, the NTC was intended as the closest possible simulation of how we would fight if hostilities ever broke out in central Europe.

LIFTING THE FOG OF WAR

A simple illustration of the clarity the playbook provided was a major problem my company averted in the typically confusing process of moving out of an assembly area before dawn, following an evening bivouac. Because the plays defined where each individual tank and armored fighting vehicle would generally position in the battalion formation, it greatly reduced the potential for confusion when something went awry. In the pitch dark during the morning of our first movement to contact at NTC, just as we began to roll, my tank's track broke, immobilizing the sixty-ton beast. I was leading the unit out of the assembly area, and the entire company halted behind my broken tank. Not wanting to break radio silence before our appointed time, I jumped off, ran to one of the other tanks in the platoon, and switched places with that tank's commander. This exercise took about three minutes, and the rest of the battalion was well ahead of us by the time I was able to check my bearings.

Nonetheless, it was straightforward to orient off the color-coded chemical light sticks that we mounted on the backs of each tank. In the distance, my new loader spotted the faint blue glowing lights of Bravo Company. No one had to pull out the operations order to check where Bravo was supposed to be for this operation or what color light stick they were using. We already knew that, because we were conducting a movement to contact on a narrow front; Bravo was blue, and they would be ahead of us to the left. We started off at increased speed and took up our expected position in the movement play.

The lead tank for a company experiencing a maintenance issue (such as a broken track) is a representative mishap. It was pitch dark, there was no moon, and you couldn't see a thing. Without the simplicity of the playbook, we could have easily become disoriented, and an entire tank company may have been lost until daylight.

The plays served to reduce chaos in the fog of war. In the earlier example, my platoon intimately understood their role in a movement to contact. The tank commander and driver of each tank kept an eye on where the other elements in the task force were moving. Even if my tank had been taken out instead of just being down for maintenance, my platoon sergeant would have immediately jumped into the leadership of the platoon with a solid understanding of our mission and our place within the battalion's overall operation. Time after time during the NTC rotation, the playbook served as a guide through chaos and confusion. Although many contingencies were foreseen in the plays, we could not account for all the things that might go awry. When chaos erupted, every soldier's understanding of the general concept would spark initiative and facilitate crucial decision-making at all levels. The mission would go on.

INSPIRING INITIATIVE

An important part of our defensive play was to set up in decoy positions during the evening, when OPFOR scouts and reconnaissance patrols would typically discover the position of their enemy with great skill. Against most task forces, the OPFOR commanders used this precise knowledge of their enemy's position with great effect. Our play involved deceiving the OPFOR. We would stay in the decoy positions until just before the OPFOR started moving to attack. Once our scouts detected the first rumblings of the enemy columns, we would pull into our prepared positions.

During our first major defensive mission at NTC, Alpha Company's (my company) decoy was foiled when nearly half our tanks experienced maintenance problems and could not move from the decoy positions. We were sitting ducks. The waterlogged tanks fought as best they could, but the OPFOR knew precisely where they sat. OPFOR managed to bypass most of Alpha Company or knock them out with concentrated artillery fire. For a moment, it became apparent that they were likely to break through and win the battle; the 9–0 goal might go up in smoke. However the struggle was still raging, and this task force had an absolute clarity of purpose.

Because of the playbook, every platoon leader had a general grasp of the position of 4-68's forces on the battlefield. Through months of preparatory training, many had developed an intuitive sense of the flow of a battle. When desperate reports came in that OPFOR elements had bypassed Alpha Company, soldiers throughout the other companies knew what that meant: The enemy would be rolling into the heart of the task force's position. The playbook told the other commanders and platoon leaders where our vulnerabilities would lie. They did not have to think about the specific defensive scheme; it was all part of the defensive play.

Communication was chaotic. Little seemed to be happening along the rest of the front. Dibella and the other commanders knew the regiment was engaging Alpha Company, but it was unclear how dire our situation was. The OPFOR started to mass for a breakthrough by going around the remnants of Alpha. On the battalion command net, Alpha Commander Dave Carruthers's last call was to notify everyone that Alpha Company was down. It was our most desperate moment.

In an inspired act of valor, fellow platoon leader Bobby Campbell took the initiative. Responding to vague information about the OPFOR's avenue of attack, the aggressive Texan charged his platoon toward the alternate position he had scouted as part of the defensive play. With all guns blazing, Campbell's platoon surprised the OPFOR. Campbell's concentrated fire slowed the enemy, giving the task force desperately needed minutes to respond. Dibella called in everything we had left, combining fierce air support, well-timed artillery fire, and every tank-killing asset that could close on the slowed OPFOR columns. As the task force massed lethal firepower, the OPFOR juggernaut finally halted. After a few minutes of this intense defensive rally, MILES kill lights were lit up throughout the simulated Soviet formation. The OPFOR had been stopped in its tracks. Because he knew the play and had drilled it and practiced it multiple times, all Campbell needed was an inkling that Alpha Company had been bypassed. He knew what to do even without clear instructions.

Campbell recalled the battle thirty years later. "We were the task force reserve. All we did was react. The challenge was moving forward enough to be able to engage the enemy without running straight into them and getting slaughtered. Really, it became more of a movement to contact at the platoon level, so that we didn't become decisively engaged. Once we established contact, we still had to present a retrograde fight. We couldn't stand toe-to-toe and slug it out with them. We had to keep them at our max range, and I think that's what bought the task force the time to reposition."

This turned the tide in what would go down in Silver Lion history as our closest battle. Bobby's heroic execution of a playbook contingency brought us to victory. Achieving the 9–0 goal was still possible.

Some would contend that a playbook could make your unit become predictable to an enemy over time. To those detractors, I would say look again at football's wishbone offense. The defending team knows the play you are going to run 70 percent of the time. The triple option is coming, either to the right or to the left. You are lined up with three backs in the backfield as plain as day. There is nothing fancy or razzle-dazzle about the wishbone offense; it is about blocking and tackling—crisp execution of a well-designed play. It is about discipline; every member of the team must be absolutely prepared for their assignment. Great teams have used the wishbone to win Division I collegiate championships. Army's team had their best seasons in years after converting to the wishbone.

Back at the auditorium briefing, nine months prior to the NTC deployment, Dibella had anticipated these kinds of heroics. As a battle ensues, chaos and confusion inevitably enter the scene; weapon systems break down; the enemy reacts unexpectedly; rain, mist, mud, and snow obscure vision; contradictory reports come from all sectors; situational assessments are sparse and inaccurate; communications become jammed and garbled, and contact is lost with critical friendly personnel; enemy deceptions and decoys confound the situation; soldiers are killed. Understanding what is actually happening in the middle of a battle and making the right decisions has been one of the greatest challenges of military command since the first caveman took up a club. For Dibella, in these confused situations clarity was critical, and the playbook was there to provide it.

Following our success, the Army latched on to the playbook concept. It has helped countless units become more proficient in their combat operations and undoubtedly saved many American lives. However, too often our success at NTC was misrepresented as being a result simply of the playbook. The playbook was only a part—albeit a significant part—of a larger transformation that was happening within the Silver Lions. The playbook worked not just because the plays were well conceived; it worked because it was the outgrowth of the maniacal obsession to defeat the OPFOR and the incredible volcano of creativity that happened in the task force.

3

STRUCTURING

4-68 TO FOCUS

ON THE PURPOSE

Nearly every organization debates between centralization and decentralization. In oversimplified and general terms, the decentralization advocates put their faith in individuals and in an invisible hand guided by self-motivated, self-interested people who maximize collective output by acting in their own best interests. Contrasting this, centralization advocates believe that the self-interest of the individual can be insidious and will not drive maximal results. For centralization advocates, maximizing the effectiveness of systems and processes within the organization requires the direction of astute, well-educated planners, guided by collaborative leaders who stand above the everyday fray and make informed decisions with a higher-level perspective. It is these highly tuned processes that will then lead to sustainable results.

Proponents of either approach argue their side as if life itself depended on the outcome.

Task Force 4-68 essentially stood above this debate. Dibella structured the organization to win every battle at the NTC; nothing else mattered. The organizational structure reflected his sense of how lines of authority should be drawn, first and foremost, for maximal effectiveness in combat and, second, for effectiveness in training and preparation. The unit's structure was built around an expectation (that grew into a culture) of accountability at every level. On one hand, it was highly decentralized: Commanders and others were given great freedom to develop their own operating procedures, to experiment with different approaches in training and preparation, and to devise their team's command and control methods. Inasmuch as any military unit can be decentralized, Task Force 4-68 was. Yet on the other hand, Dibella also inspired and expected an exceptional level of teamwork and cooperation between his decentralized companies and their supporting units.

DECENTRALIZED TEAMWORK

When it came to both the formal and informal lines of authority, it was crystal clear that the commanders directly facing the enemy would benefit by having every possible resource available to them. They were the leaders on the front line, and Dibella aligned all other parts of the organization to support them. The primary mission of the battalion staff was to support the commanders.

Bravo Company commander Joe Moore related an incident in which one member of the battalion S4 (supply and logistics) shop was not responding to Bravo Company's request for certain supplies needed for a training mission. Providing the supplies would disrupt preparations for an upcoming supply-room inspection.

Dibella became aware of the incident. In a calculated rage, he stormed out of his office and made it clear to everyone in the S4 shop that they were there to get the company commanders what they needed for training. They would not be heroes for maximizing control of the supply shop or having the prettiest logistical paperwork. It was their job to get the units in the field the matériel, food, fuel, and ammunition they needed. All the systems and internal controls of the supply shop should have been set up to do this. They could and should work to optimize their ability to do exactly that, but never at the expense of those on the front. Dibella made it simple and absolutely clear to the battalion staff that when issues arose, the company commanders were in charge.

At the same time, Dibella would not allow the commanders to abuse their authority. The systems and processes of the battalion staff mattered. No commander could get away with being unresponsive to a process the staff developed to ensure they could provide the best support. For example, Bravo Company's consistent tardiness delivering training schedules that the S3 (operations and training staff) needed to ensure effective coordination of the overall training for the task force was unacceptable.

Moore recounted, "Dibella told me I was letting him and the rest of the battalion down. It was devastating to hear that from someone I respected so much. I felt as if I had just slapped my own grandmother."

Bravo Company never delivered another late training schedule.

Teamwork was of such critical importance to achieving the battalion's purpose that Dibella went to great lengths to ensure that all the commanders understood how it would affect the career-essential ratings on their Officer Efficiency Reports (OERs). As he explained it, when officers completed their support forms in preparation for the review, "they better have a lot of team-building stuff in there. They should be asking, *'What am I doing to build a team at my level, and what am doing to contribute to the higher level team?'*"

For the company commanders, he was clear: "Do something great to build your company team—A minus. Do something great in your company and share it with another company openly—A. Do something great in your company and share it with another company and not make a big deal out of it; share because you know it is the right thing to do—A+. That third type of commander is a team builder, the kind you want to promote."

Although a company or even a single platoon might sometimes make the difference in a particular battle, the only score that ultimately mattered was that of the task force. The absolutely clear goal of a 9–0 victory clarified the overriding importance of teamwork and making every company and platoon the best they could be. Certainly each company commander wanted their company recognized as the best, and each platoon leader wanted their team to rank the highest. We were a fiercely competitive bunch, but our clear purpose forced us to approach competitiveness within the task force in the fashion of many highly effective families or sports teams: You wanted to outdo your teammate, score a few more points, or grab more rebounds, but you also wanted your teammate to have their best possible game. Dibella's informal OER system expounded on that philosophy.

4

ORGANIZING AROUND
STRENGTHS IN 4-68

Task Force 4-68 organized for its mission outside of Army doctrine in two ways: The first was our belief in the playbook as a method of command, control, and mission dissemination for combat operations. The second was our structure. Dibella did not believe that all men do all things well, and he felt it was foolhardy to ask them to do so. We developed the plays and roles for each subunit around the strengths of its leaders (commissioned and noncommissioned). This statement is crucial for any leader to understand if they decide to use a playbook concept. Our organizational structure worked for many reasons, but first and foremost it worked because it was developed and built around strengths.

This approach was a significant departure from conventional wisdom at the time. It was not until the later 1990s that Donald Clifton of Gallup would advance the concept of a strengths-based leadership approach into the modern mainstream. Most organizations—and certainly the Army at the time—were not conscious of the advantages this style could bring.

For example, the Army personnel (human resources) system expected that officers essentially be masters of all trades. Promotions below the zone (for top performers) would be granted only to those who had top-block (best among their peer group) ratings in every job they had. Policies, procedures, and doctrine were consistent with this attitude. Significant promotion opportunities required an officer to have a broad range of roles and to excel in all of them.

From Fred Dibella's viewpoint, officers who could do it all were very rare. Being great as an S4, awesome as a tactical officer at the military academy, or effectively leading troops in combat called on different strengths. The well-rounded approach would overlook some who were truly exceptional at certain roles but weak in others. Truly talented combat commanders might be passed over for promotion because they had not excelled in a staff position at the Pentagon. Only during wartime, when the situation was dire, would the Army personnel system recognize the difference between effectiveness as a staff officer and effectiveness as a combat commander. George S. Patton Jr. is perhaps the most shining example of these extremes. His daring, aggressive combat leadership was essential for breaking the Allied forces out of the Normandy beachhead, but few would find him useful as a Pentagon staff officer.

Dibella inherited a battalion that was in pretty bad shape. I came to 4-68 just as he was about to arrive. Other officers and NCOs talked with some measure of discontent and even shame about the shape of the unit prior to his arrival. We were generally considered to be the worst unit in the division. The previous commander and executive officer were essentially relieved of command (fired, to translate into business parlance). It was not a high-performance organization. It was an organization recovering from a dysfunctional command with a below-average performance history and low morale. LTC Dibella would not have the challenge of taking a good unit to the next level; it was a true turnaround.

Dibella immediately began discerning the strengths of the unit's soldiers and leaders, looking to maximize them. This strengths analysis became intimately connected with the plays we developed for the playbook. Early in the process, as we began dissecting the experience of other units at NTC, three principles arose that became clear elements for victory:

1. Win the reconnaissance–counterreconnaissance battle.
2. Hit the flank.
3. Mass at decisive points and times.

Bravo 4-68 Armor had several NTC veterans, including its company commander Joe Moore, who had been a battalion S3 (operations) during a rotation. These veterans were experienced, cool under fire, and good with land-navigation skills. They knew the NTC battlefields from previous experience and were outstanding at handling chaos. They seemed to thrive in confused situations and were exceptional at bringing order to that confusion. Bravo became the natural choice to lead the task force in movement operations and in the attacks on an objective. They also knew how to hit the flank.

Charlie Company was one of the attached mechanized infantry companies from 2-8 Infantry Battalion. They were innovative, energetic, flexible, and good in a mounted role. These were exactly the kinds of strengths that would be handy in a recon–counterrecon role. Outmaneuvering and outsmarting enemy reconnaissance elements was crucial, and the soldiers of this unit loved such a challenge.

The other tank company Alpha (my parent unit) had a competitive commander, Dave Carruthers, who loved to kill enemy tanks. We also had many of the best long-range tank gunnery experts in the battalion. Every platoon had at least one senior tank commander who had graduated from the elite master gunnery school. We were like a unit filled with *American Sniper* clones, wielding 105-millimeter guns mounted to sixty-ton mobile platforms. If the enemy moved in front of the guns of

Alpha Company, one of fourteen highly lethal tank main guns would find them in their sights and take them out. In addition to long-range tank gunnery, Alpha had a knack for finding the best positions to shoot from, capitalizing on the contours of the terrain. Alpha Company was the central killing power of the task force; our plays were designed to get Alpha in position to do that killing.

The second mechanized infantry unit was actually Bravo Company 2-8 Infantry. We renamed them Delta Force to avoid confusion with the Bravo tank company. A commander who was a physical-training enthusiast led this unit, and he drove the company to have excellent physical strength and endurance. They were exceptional in a dismounted role—rock-hard infantrymen who could go deep into an enemy defensive position. We knew that if we could infiltrate with dismounted infantry, it would have a shocking effect, and we designed key elements of the offensive plays to capitalize on this strength.

As Dibella would say, the intent was to give the enemy defenders two choices: stay in their holes and be killed by Delta Force's dismounted infantry and their antitank weaponry, or get out of their holes and be killed by the highly accurate guns of Alpha Company and the determined attack of Bravo Company's tanks.

The strengths-based approach also filtered down to the platoons. I was the leader of First Platoon Alpha Company. With considerable coaching from Casey Jones, the company first sergeant, I had developed a strong ability to decode contour terrain maps. My platoon led the company out of the assembly area for every offensive operation.

A basic course instructor would argue that every lieutenant should experience leading the company formation out of assembly. What if I was killed or missing—who would lead? We discarded that idea and allowed each platoon leader to develop as much as they could, with our limited training time and resources, in their platoon's primary mission according to the playbook. Focusing on those things you or your unit were most likely to be called to do was a force multiplier. It was about going deep and mastering your part in the play. You would learn the responsibilities of the other platoon leaders by watching them excel.

PURPOSEFUL STRUCTURE IN ACTION

My two rotations as a platoon leader fighting the OPFOR at the NTC illustrate how the playbook, decentralized teamwork, and strengths-based organization work together. In the first rotation, my platoon had been cross-attached to another battalion to fill out its ranks. We trained for about six weeks with this other unit and then traveled with them to the NTC. The other unit's task force did not have a playbook, but the operations staff was highly versed in the methodology of the Army, which taught battalions to follow a very well-researched nine-step planning process to develop their operations orders on receipt of a mission from higher headquarters. This process is a case study in analysis and decision-making. It is very well thought out and highly logical. The only problem—and it is an Achilles' heel—is that it takes too long.

At about 11:00 p.m. on the evening preceding one coordinated attack during that first rotation, I received notification of the platoon's reassignment to a different tank company. We woke any sleeping members of the platoon and, on a moonless night, started up the tanks to make way to the new company. This was in the days before GPS, and there were no landmarks to help guide our route—just a point to get to on the map. Since final orders were not out yet, I had no knowledge of where the other assets of the task force were positioned.

Repositioning was an odyssey. We ran across one of the maintenance units, one of the mechanized infantry companies, a group of Observer–Controllers, and some unexpected formations of concertina wire before finally pulling into the new company assembly area under the guiding light of the company first sergeant's flashlight.

After parking our tanks, I made my way to the company commander's tank to get the orders for the mission that was to begin in about five hours. The company commander's gunner was awake in the tank. He told me the commander was trying to get some sleep before battalion called him to a meeting to disseminate the order. That call had not yet come. It was about 1:30 a.m. when I returned to my tank. All I could tell the platoon was that we would be on the offensive tomorrow (really, later that morning) and that we would move out at 0600.

The next thing I remember was my gunner waking me up on my favorite left front fender of the tank at 0530, telling me there were still no orders. I got on the landline and asked the company commander about the situation. He essentially said that the orders were on the way and that we needed to be ready to move at 0600. At about 0545, I received notice to report to the CO's tank; he had copies of the orders. After he gave us the best explanation he could in five minutes, all the platoon leaders rushed back to their platoons.

It was 0600 when I got back to my cupola—time to move. I yelled to the tank commanders that I had the orders and would disseminate them over the radio once we had passed the line of departure and radio silence was lifted. Needless to say, that operation ended as a total OPFOR victory over us.

That experience compared to my 4-68 rotation was like night and day. The playbook facilitated decentralized control and helped ensure that the companies and platoons had adequate planning time for the next mission.

As Tom Piskel, the Silver Lion S3 (operations officer), explained it, "Our job, once we received the mission from higher HQ, was to get the operations orders done, call the commanders in, rehearse the operation, and get the commanders back to their units within two hours. At NTC, we did this every time. The playbook made it all possible."

As an aside, there was a tremendous amount of work and ingenuity that Piskel and his team poured into meeting that two-hour requirement, which we will cover later. Without the framework of the playbook, decentralized teamwork, and strength-based structure of the battalion, however, it would never have been possible.

The battalion headquarters for that first rotation took most of the time between missions to develop what they believed was a near-perfect plan. They followed the nine-step planning process, refined and optimized the plan, and then disseminated it to the combat units once it was complete. The centralized focus of this series of steps was to develop the best overall plan.

Remember, Task Force 4-68 used a wishbone offense. Our plan only required tweaking one of six plays, which the battalion had developed together over eleven months. The focus was to get the order out of the battalion headquarters so the companies and platoons would have time to disseminate, rehearse, and prepare for the mission. The frontline soldiers could conduct a reconnaissance of the position, carry out map-based drills, review the elements of executing the play, and take other actions to help them prepare. It was decentralized, with two-thirds of the preparation time below the battalion headquarters level. In this fashion, the decentralization of power was, counterintuitively, an important part of providing the absolutely clear central purpose to the organization.

5

4-68'S UNWAVERING

SUPPORT FROM THE TOP

CEOs and other senior leaders who want the benefits of a focused structure have to be vehement and consistent in their support of it. Conflicting priorities will arise; how each of these is handled will set many wheels in motion, cause some wheels to stop, and cause some wheels in motion or at rest to remain in their current state. The decisions a higher-level leader makes to resolve the inevitable conflict between support and line units will send strong messages throughout the larger unit. Such decisions clarify priorities and set precedents. The unit's leaders will know the relative standing between line and support. Dibella was unequivocally in support of the decentralized, combat-mission-focused structure; the power rested with the trigger pullers.

Shortly after his arrival at Fort Carson, LTC Dibella had an introductory meeting with Fourth Mechanized Infantry Division's commanding general. He recalls the meeting as if it happened yesterday:

"Major General Bartlett wanted to ensure that I understood his priorities for battalion commanders. He gave me a three-word mission statement. It was very simple. 'Win at NTC!' To emphasize the point, the general said, 'If that is not clear, let me state it another way: Beat the OPFOR! Any questions?'"

Dibella would respond in what he later described as one of his more enlightened moments, "No, sir. Absolutely clear."

The new battalion commander and the division's top leader would have further conversations about priorities in command. Major General (MG) Bartlett went on to elaborate that there would be many demands that would detract from this primary mission, even things that come down from his office. He expected his battalion commanders to figure out how to keep those activities most crucial to combat readiness at the top of the priority list.

Dibella talked about one of the important pieces of advice MG Bartlett gave him, "He used to say, 'Get in the middle. On the things that are not primary to your mission, just get in the middle. Don't try to be on the top, or it will take too much effort away from the important things. Don't be on the bottom, or I'll have to send in the G1 or someone else and that will distract you.'"

The point of the advice was to stay focused on the most important things; just be average on the things that don't contribute. That way, you won't distract your attention or attract the attention of others. You don't want help fixing unimportant things; such help would only distract your attention from those activities and actions that will help achieve the purpose.

The conversation with MG Bartlett was liberating for Dibella. The major general essentially gave the LTC a hall pass on the conflicting demands that would detract from the mission. Dibella took the conversation to heart and decided to trust this general, and as a result, 4-68 was hopelessly average while marching on the parade field but stellar on the battlefield.

Many leaders say one thing about priorities, but their actions speak differently. Major General Bartlett was not one of these leaders. He meant what he said and proved it several times in the lead-up to the

NTC rotation. This level of trust and support at the very top of the divisional chain of command was absolutely critical to the task force's success. Many things Dibella and the task force did in preparation for the rotation were outside of normal Army doctrine. Some were in direct opposition to that doctrine. Without the support and the overall command environment at Fourth Mechanized Infantry Division, it is not likely that Dibella would have been able to influence the task force as he did.

When MG Bartlett spoke of "winning at NTC" or "beating the OPFOR," he understood that it was not an end in itself; rather, it was a means to an end. He issued that goal because he realized that if a combat battalion can somehow manage to train well enough to beat the vaunted OPFOR, they would have to be singularly obsessed with becoming combat ready. Being ready to win the nation's wars is, after all, why combat units exist. If you can beat the OPFOR, you must have mastered the arts of gunnery, maintenance, fitness, stamina, maneuvering, fire support, personnel replacement, and so many other skills.

In a briefing following the rotation, Dibella emphasized, "If you do not master all of the combat skills necessary on the modern battlefield, the skilled and experienced OPFOR will quickly discover your weaknesses and terminally punish you."

When a leader challenges the status quo and the expectations of most of his or her subordinates, there are common reactions within those being led. Three distinct groups typically arise: (1) A small minority embraces change and new ideas. They become energized and work to help drive the changes. (2) Another often-influential group opposes change. They question decisions and may even work to persuade others that change is dangerous or unnecessary. They may claim that it is just a fad of the new leader and that, like all fads, it will fade. (3) The majority group looks to the direction of the herd and then follows. If higher-level leadership shows anything but enthusiasm for the new ideas, the naysayer group feels empowered to fight against the change.

This fight can become insidious, and the collective energy needed to make a transition to something new can be spent working against the change instead.

Dibella also had every measure of support for what he was doing from his direct superior, Colonel Richard Davis, the Second Brigade Commander. Colonel Davis was one of the very rare senior leaders who would go to great lengths to support what his subordinate commanders were attempting to accomplish.

As Dibella explained it in a later conversation: "You see, after I explained my intended playbook concept to him, he task organized the tank and infantry battalions a year before our NTC rotation. I traded two tank companies to 2-8 Infantry, and I received two mechanized infantry companies in return. That was huge—*huge*. All the staff guys at Brigade said, 'You can't do this! How will you manage SIDPERS (the Army's computerized personnel management system), and how will you requisition parts, and where will the soldiers live, and how will they be paid, and what about OERs, and what about motor pools and tank gunnery?' Etc., etc., et-freaking-cetera. But Dick just said, 'Figure it out.' See, he realized that if I was going to have a playbook that would need to be drilled and drilled to a gnat's ass, then I needed to have a constant task organization."

One and two levels above him were leaders who wanted Dibella to win and who approached NTC with a fiercely competitive spirit, but Dibella would later lament his disdain for the kind of leader who was not out to win. Going back to the Army football analogy, he simply could not understand the opinion of some senior officers at the Academy regarding the football program. In a postretirement briefing to general officers, as Dibella was going through the impact that Army football had on our development of the playbook, he couldn't help but add an aside: "You know, there are senior officers at the Academy who actually believe that the objective of the Army football program ought to be to conform to the ideals of the military academy or to play representative Division I-A football. What the hell does that mean—to be 'representative'? The objective of the football program is to *win*. When there are two scores tallied up, you make sure yours is the higher one. Am I covering this too fast for you all?"

There were some in the military who similarly looked on the NTC experience. They felt the objective for an NTC rotation was to get some great, close-to-real-world training. You would fight against a tough opponent and learn valuable lessons. You would develop your combat and combat support systems in an intense training environment. These are all admirable goals, but there could be only one objective for Task Force 4-68's NTC rotation: to *win* every battle and score a 9–0 victory over the OPFOR.

6

CLARITY OF
PURPOSE AT STRYKER

John Brown established a very simple and measurable goal. Anyone who worked in the company during his tenure, along with the vast majority of investors, could describe that goal with a single number: 20 percent. Like Dibella's 9–0, 20 percent was simple, straightforward, measurable, and meaningful. The goal to grow earnings by 20 percent per year permeated every department and was deeply ingrained in the mindset of the company's leaders, managers, and employees. The constant awareness of the goal and the absolute need to achieve it had an impact on all aspects of the business. This laser focus led to extraordinary performance over an unprecedented twenty-eight years. For Brown, strategy, structure, and just about every facet of the business for which C-suite leaders are responsible flowed from the goal.

John Brown had the gift of saying in a few words what would require paragraphs for most. He could boil complex ideas or complicated theories down to a single sentence. In so simply and clearly defining the purpose at Stryker, Brown capitalized on this great talent.

During a 2009 interview for the local Kalamazoo newspaper, Brown remarked, "From the goal comes strategy."

This simple statement speaks volumes about his thought process. For Brown, everything flowed from the goal. The strategy, tactics, approach to product development, sales techniques, manufacturing methods, and so on were all means to achieving that goal.

Success comes with achieving a goal. This is a simple concept. At Stryker, the very idea of success had no meaning unless there was a goal around which success could be defined, and all goals were tied to the overarching purpose: 20-percent earnings growth. This purpose answered the fundamental question: *What are we trying to achieve?* While many business thinkers and business-school strategy pundits would decry John Brown's singular focus on a simple numerical goal, he would have it no other way.

Twenty-percent growth was a carefully selected pace. It stretched people. It was aggressive, but it was also a pace that the company was not looking to greatly exceed. When Brown was formulating the 20-percent goal, he was conscious of the impact growth could have on the organization. Some of the board members were pushing for 30 percent. Brown was thinking long term. Thirty percent might be possible for a year or two, but he did not believe the organization could support it over the long haul.

In our 2015 interview, Brown recalled, "When I announced the 20 percent, one of the directors said, 'We were thinking in terms of thirty.' I said, 'I can't do thirty. We think twenty is phenomenal.'"

Twenty percent was a constant and consistent goal. Author Jim Collins expertly discusses the resolute power in Stryker's not-too-little, not-too-much "20-mile march" as he termed it in his book *Great by Choice*. I believe, as does John Brown, that Collins describes that attribute quite accurately. Brown used the metric to define the kind of enterprise Stryker would be. To provide a constant reminder, it became a requirement not just for the year but also for each quarter. There would be no "slow" quarter that could be "caught up" in the future. The 20-percent goal was constant, and it required unwavering vigilance.

John Brown's style was more subdued than Fred Dibella's onstage proclamation. Nonetheless, the impact was just as pervasive, and Brown had a much longer time to drive home the message. He used virtually every available tool and technique to inculcate the ethos throughout the company. He began by directly and confidently stating the goal over and over again. He stated it publicly; he stated it at shareholder meetings; he stated it in internal management meetings; he stated it at employee presentations and ceremonies; he stated it to prospective new hires.

When he interviewed me, it was very clear: "We are a growth company. We set the goal at 20 percent per year."

In a way, 20-percent growth came to be a screener for potential employees. It was commonly known throughout the local community that Stryker people worked very hard and had high standards to meet. If growing at such a rate was not something that excited you or if you felt that striving for a number was not inspirational enough, working at Stryker would not be a good fit. In contrast, the well-known requirement served to attract those who might be inspired by it.

Brown later recalled this effect of the goal: "The demands were very high, and it took a unique personality to fit in. It took people who had a burning ambition to be successful."

Twenty percent became intimately ingrained in every aspect of the business. If you spent an hour at any Stryker facility, you would leave knowing that the company's overarching goal was 20-percent growth. Like Dibella's 9–0, every employee knew the goal, understood its overriding importance, and believed they could in some way affect its achievement. Twenty percent became a rally cry for nearly everything. If a customer service team was going to work on improving their answer rate, a 20-percent improvement would be the goal. Operations managers would set 20 percent as the goal for inventory reduction programs. Sales managers all knew their quota for the next year would be a 20-percent increase over the prior year. Facility managers who wanted to cut a particular cost would target a 20-percent reduction. Customer satisfaction surveys would target 20-percent improvement goals. Assembly team leaders would target a 20-percent improvement in throughput from a line redesign. Twenty percent was everywhere and in every activity.

7

CLARITY OF

PURPOSE IN ACTION

AT STRYKER

During the early 1990s, the largest public corporation in Kalamazoo, Michigan, was pharmaceutical giant Upjohn. Following the decline of the paper mill industry, Upjohn had kept Kalamazoo on the national business map during the 1970s and 1980s. Nonetheless, reporters for the local paper were intrigued by what was happening at Stryker.

"Can so many people really be that obsessed with growth?" they wondered.

One Sunday article highlighted Stryker with a headline like "Not the Biggest in Town, But the Best."

Those inside Stryker often teased their Upjohn friends when local rumors spread that John Brown was being considered for Upjohn's CEO position. We joked that the Upjohn faithful who always seemed to have the time for all kinds of community activities would gain a whole new concept of their work-life balance. As Stryker's growth continued, the company earned a reputation as a very well-managed organization with highly streamlined internal processes and an untiring workforce. This reputation reflected the truth.

Budget planning was very simple: Use the ingenuity, creativity, drive, talents, and abilities of all your people to deliver at least 20-percent growth over your previous year's numbers and to prepare for 20-percent growth in the years to come. No manager or leader would expend an ounce of energy thinking about setting a goal for any important activity below a 20-percent improvement from the prior year's result. The power of this simplicity was absolutely magical. In the years following Brown's retirement, as the 20-percent requirement was relaxed, division presidents and financial officers spent countless hours positioning and politicking for their budget targets in the upcoming year. During Brown's era, this process was simple and straightforward; the 20-percent goal provided absolute clarity, and no amount of politicking would change it.

MATCHING INCENTIVES TO THE PURPOSE

Reinforcing the annual budget goal, Brown capitalized on multiple methodologies to ensure that the 20-percent goal became part of the very DNA of the organization. Bonuses, awards, competitive comparisons, high-level recognition, and the standing of business units within the internal hierarchy were all based on growth, with 20 percent as the benchmark.

For example, most managers and leaders at Stryker had an annual bonus as part of their compensation package. During Brown's era, a bonus package represented a larger percentage of total compensation than was typical for employees at comparable medical-device companies. The bonus structure was a key tool to inculcate the passion to deliver growth. At the highest level, the bonus plans were simple and straightforward. Division presidents would have a variety of financial objectives, but the vast weight of the bonus was based on achieving the division's earnings goal. The formula used for earnings and most other financial goals was coined the *growth formula*. It would begin paying out only if the results exceed last year's numbers. It was uncapped.

$$\frac{actual\ result - prior\ year\ result}{prior\ year\ result \times 0.2} \times \quad \begin{array}{c} target\ bonus\ amount \\ in\ dollars \end{array}$$

As a more specific example, with $10,000 as the target, this line of the bonus would pay $0 if the year's result came in equal to or below last year's. At 10-percent growth, the bonus line would pay out at $5,000. At 20 percent, the bonus line would pay its full target amount of $10,000. There were no caps to the upside, so if results were 40 percent above last year, the payout would be $20,000. Exceeding a goal during a year was a great way to maximize income. However, the downside was that the formula for next year would be based off the blowout from the current year. In the philosophy of the bonus program and the company, 20-percent growth was a short-, intermediate-, and long-term goal. One-hit wonders were not the heroes at Stryker; consistent excellent performance over time was the goal.

The point of the process was to constantly reinforce the idea that growth is the important thing. Leaders and managers applied the growth formula to goals for major efforts throughout the corporation. For several years, I led interdisciplinary teams focused on manufactured-product cost reduction. As you might guess, the stretch goal for the teams was to reduce costs by 20 percent, so we based the team's bonus formula on that 20-percent improvement. The formula could apply to nearly every measurable goal, and if the goal was not measurable, it did not belong in the bonus plan.

The Stryker growth formula was simple and cogent. It defined the expected outcome: There is no bonus paid for a result that did not improve from the prior year. With bonuses as such a significant part of the total compensation package, the message was doubly clear: We pay for growth. The target mattered to the employees and their teams, their pride, and their sense of achievement. It mattered to their personal finances and even to their prospects for continued employment.

KEEPING IT SIMPLE

At its core, the *Silver Lions Playbook* was a method of simplifying the complex task of battalion-level combat operations. Success would not come from devising an ingenious plan for each battle but from hard work in executing the six simple plays that relied on disciplined execution. Units and subunits would become experts at performing their roles. Stryker also kept its fundamental approach very simple through the relentless pursuit of 20-percent growth. As management fads bloomed and withered over its twenty-eight-year growth history, Stryker kept true to its straightforward philosophy of business.

Brown summarized this eloquently in the 1994 annual report and in multiple internal presentations: "All our divisions must excel in three fundamental areas: product development, manufacturing, and sales. Our management mantra is *Invent it, make it, sell it.*"

He would restate and expound on this, emphasizing that Stryker's key to success is a simple approach combined with a lot of hard work. "If we invent the best products, have the best salespeople in each respective market selling them, and deliver them to the customer at high quality and reasonable cost, it's likely we will continue to win and grow 20 percent every year."

This unpretentious mantra—*invent it, make it, sell it*—was a further instrument of clarity. The mantra did not encourage managers or leaders to follow the latest fads or develop intricate plans to outwit the competition. Instead, the emphasis was on executing the basics with excellence. Like the wishbone offense, which relies on toughness, precision in execution, and unit cohesion, Stryker divisions would deliver growth by highly tuned execution in R&D, manufacturing, and sales. There was nothing fancy or ingenious about it, but when executed methodically by fanatical teams, sustainable, excellent performance was the result.

John Brown reflected on the advantages of such simplicity in our 2015 conversation: "I believe that if you've got to read a document to know how you are going to operate, I think you are in trouble. What I think you want to do is put it in the head and in the heart, and if you do that, success will continue. For the goals, compliance issues, innovation, the simpler you can make it, the better off you're going to be. Communicate it to the organization, and it's just phenomenal how well that works."

Human beings struggle to internalize a twenty-page—or even a two-page—mission statement, but they can wrap their heads around a three-word overarching purpose and simple supporting mantras emphasizing the significance of those primary tasks essential to achieving it. Such simple communications were easy to remember and uncomplicated to repeat. As a result, they spread quickly and generally reached every person in the organization. People who never read the annual reports or attended Brown's presentations knew about the goal and the mantra.

MONTHLY REVIEWS

An important part of this straightforward emphasis on the basics was monthly reviews. In the early years, before separating into divisions, these would be for the *invent it, make it, and sell it* arms of the business. As the company spawned into many different divisions, Brown kept a similar structure in place. Every month, the divisional leadership—the general manager, financial officer, human resources leader, and the leader of R&D (*invent it*); operations and quality (*make it*); and sales, marketing, customer service (*sell it*)—would attend a meeting with John Brown and the corporate CFO. This financial review would cover detailed assessments of actions under way in each part of the business driving growth. It would include a progress report on major R&D efforts, improvement efforts in quality or manufacturing, and marketing initiatives.

In keeping with the core philosophy, those closest to the customer received the most attention. A majority of the time would be spent conducting an exhaustive review of the sales performance for each region and each individual sales rep. Just as Dibella ensured the battalion staff and all other parts of the organization were lined up to support the combat leaders on the front line, Brown ensured the sales team received full support from those in the home office and manufacturing facilities.

A CHART FOR EVERY SALESPERSON

Each region and every rep had a chart showing their territory sales and the past history. Divisional sales leaders would go through every chart with the CEO. Those reps whose plots went up and to the right were the heroes; their sales were growing. Reps showing a flat or declining graph were the subjects of scrutiny. If they had a history of high performance, they would be allowed some grace time to turn the trend around, but Stryker generally demonstrated little patience for those with no history of excellence. The financial reviews were a key part of the culture of accountability that arose from the drive for growth, and they epitomized Stryker's emphasis on business fundamentals.

Being a sales rep at Stryker was like being a member of an ultracompetitive world-championship track or swimming team. Although the ultimate goal was for the team to rack up 20-percent sales growth—and team dynamics were critical in this—individual reps would thrive or wither on their own results. It was a high-risk, high-reward environment, where the reps were skilled hunters who essentially ate what they killed and only what they killed—100-percent straight commission, direct sales. With most reps earning about 10-percent commission on everything they sold, there were many years in which the compensation for the top salesperson in the corporation significantly exceeded that of the CEO. On the other hand, those who did not bring in the orders would only scrape by on a subsistence income, and they would not be long on the team if they did not turn their sales around.

I joined the company as a project manager in R&D, operations, and quality assurance, along with support for marketing and sales. Cutting my teeth in the *invent it* and *make it* sides of the business, it wasn't until I attended my first national sales meeting that I truly began to understand how the company worked. The sales teams were the soldiers fighting at the front, engaging the enemy (our competitors), and doing everything they could to bring in the orders. Nearly every activity in the home office was orchestrated to help the sales reps be successful. While the expectations for performance were clearly on the shoulders of the reps, the expectations that they would receive world-class support were on the shoulders of everyone else in the company.

As with complete victory over the NTC's OPFOR, Stryker's absolutely clear goal of 20-percent growth drove the company for twenty-eight years to perform in the top 1 percent of the top 1 percent. The purpose was simple and easy to understand, and Stryker's straightforward approach to its achievement was focused on vigorously executing the basic activities of a business: Invent great products and services that customers want and need. Make these products on time and of high quality. Sell them through highly motivated sales teams. Do these things with excellence. It was not complicated, but it led to amazing success.

8

STRUCTURING
STRYKER TO FOCUS
ON THE PURPOSE

John Brown's leadership at Stryker lasted much longer than the one year Fred Dibella had to prepare for the NTC rotation; in that extra time, there was greater opportunity for the organizational structure to evolve. Stryker was also unconstrained by the imposition of a defined military hierarchy. Nonetheless, the critical themes at each stage were quite similar. First and foremost, the structure served to drive home the purpose of the organization. Second, like Dibella, John Brown ensured that authority was pushed down to the lowest level. For TF 4-68, those in direct contact with the enemy knew best what was actually happening; their lives were at stake, and the resources of the task force rallied appropriately. Even though the free enterprise system did not involve imminent danger, Stryker adopted a similar approach. Those in direct contact with the customer knew the situational reality best, and great resources rallied around the salespeople to help them succeed. To put this sales-focused philosophy on steroids, Brown also laser focused the firm by creating a fiercely decentralized business unit structure.

A proper beginning of the decentralization discussion is to review some history. In the 1980s, after several years of consistently growing earnings by 20 percent, Stryker underwent a significant transformation. In later years, Brown would describe this transition from a centralized model to one based on focus through decentralization.

He recounted his epiphany: "It became obvious that *I* was the biggest obstacle to continuing 20-percent growth in the company."

Hearing this with the benefit of hindsight, many might speculate that Brown was being somewhat facetious and perhaps even displaying false modesty, but John Brown absolutely meant what he said. As the company sales grew, its leaders found that central control was not creating an environment that naturally maximized the opportunities needed for growth.

FOCUS THROUGH DECENTRALIZATION

Over time, Brown became convinced that highly engaged divisional teams, laser focused on their customer's needs, listening to their focused sales teams battling on the front lines, creating their new products, improving their processes, and creating their future would bring the energy and enthusiasm essential to achieving growth year after year. Seeking maximum growth, the company split into divisions, installed division presidents to lead them, and—in the span of less than three years—had nearly all the business processes and functions focused in the divisions.

This first split started what became a zealous drive for focus through decentralization. Nearly all of the thought process behind focusing in such a fashion spawned from the desire to make the goal of 20-percent growth absolutely clear and visible at every level. As Brown would note in the 1985 annual report, "Stryker's new structure will bring . . . effective decision-making at the lowest practicable level—and closest to the point where our opportunities and problems arise."

The first separation into semi-independent divisions occurred as the company grew toward $100 million in sales. Stryker had become involved in several widely separate markets. It had product lines that served different customers within the hospital; products that had fundamentally different manufacturing processes; and products with service, support, and delivery processes that were markedly dissimilar. The company had reached a point where the mental capacity of a leadership team to consider the bona fide opportunities in such separate markets would naturally lead to emphasis on what the team considered its best options. It would be logical to focus on the largest opportunities for the collective business.

Most companies of similar size take such an approach; it makes intuitive sense and is simple to argue. It is safe and will likely lead to good results. For Stryker, however, good was simply not enough. The company had to deliver 20-percent growth, and this safe path would likely neglect important opportunities. Continual growth required initiatives in nearly all the company's significant markets and product lines. This required choosing a more challenging path and building a structure that maintained customer focus in every major product line.

The company initially split into three operating units—Medical, Surgical, and Osteonics. The actual break was between Medical and Surgical; Osteonics was an implant manufacturing firm Stryker acquired in 1979, which was essentially independent from the start. In the breakup, Medical would include the traditional Circ-o-lectric bed, hospital stretchers, and other patient-support and treatment platforms. These were large devices that were used primarily by nurses and patients in departments throughout the hospital. Surgical comprised the patented Stryker cast cutter and a burgeoning surgical instruments product line of small handheld devices for the surgeon's use during mostly orthopedic procedures, along with a recently developed surgical optics technology.

In what would become a recurring pattern, Medical and Surgical first split the sales and marketing organizations, then followed with R&D. Sales and marketing were the primary customer-facing elements of the business, and the focused teams would develop greater intimacy with their customers. Capitalizing on this intimacy very soon involved the research and development organizations; over time, the engineers built deep relationships with thought leaders in their markets and endeavored to become experts in technologies that served them. Following this break came manufacturing, customer service, and eventually nearly every support function, including accounting, human resources, and logistics.

Brown described the split in Stryker's 1984 annual report: "Beginning in 1985, we will have three semiautonomous operating units, each responsible for designing, manufacturing, and selling its own products in the US market."

Decentralization brought several significant advantages that were all drivers of growth. In a 2004 interview for the *Kalamazoo Gazette*, Brown described his reasoning: "Our officers running the divisions get to enjoy the same excitement and pleasure of running their own business that I did, because we gave them an awful lot of autonomy. That has really paid huge dividends over the years."

As the split progressed, independent financial statements for each division helped clarify their individual contributions. The firtst statements for the newly divided Medical and Surgical businesses revealed a great deal about the viability of the surgical-instrument business and the direction it was headed.

Si Johnson, who would lead the instruments business to astounding success for over a decade, recalled the situation at later internal meetings: "We discovered that we had a highly profitable stretcher business and, at best, a break-even surgical-instruments business."

The superb profitability of the stretcher line was holding up the rest of the company. When the financial reports delineated the clear results for the two businesses, it was as if the tide had gone out, exposing the rocks at the bottom of the lake. The surgical business, while an engine for top-line growth, was not delivering earnings.

Sweeping changes were brought about that would never have happened without the split. Within a few years Instruments became an earnings driver. During the 1990s, the Instruments Division delivered a streak of earnings successes that would have seemed impossible right after the split. It was a shining example of the power of focus and clarity of purpose.

SPLITTING MY OWN DIVISION

In the early 1990s, I worked as the director of engineering for the Medical Division. I had teams working on product development and product improvements throughout the diversified bed and stretcher product line. We had introduced a new ICU bed that was reestablishing Stryker's position in this growing market. We launched a completely new line of emergency and recovery stretchers and were in the middle of a four-year process of proliferating the innovations and improvements from this launch throughout the specialty stretcher product line. I was also responsible for industrial engineering, and we were in a manufacturing renaissance, adding new manufacturing processes and improving our internal operations. Every day was totally engaging. I felt as if each project was like a new child that needed special attention and nurturing.

Then, one day, it changed. Brown and the Medical Division president had made the decision to split the division into a hospital bed business and a hospital stretcher business: Patient Care and Patient Handling, respectively. Each would have a division president, and sales, marketing, and R&D would split immediately. In a twenty-four-hour span, I went through an expedited five-step grieving process. At first, I couldn't believe what I was being told. Then I became angry. I had put tremendous energy into working with and building these teams. How could some of them be taken away with one decision?

As a leader, I wanted to put on a positive front for my team, but preparing for the communication process was a somber affair. We had been through many challenges together—late nights retooling a manufacturing plant, radically improving our product line, looking forward to the future. Losing members of my team was a highly emotional event; it was as if our Stryker family was splitting up. In the early afternoon, I closed my office door for a few minutes to collect my thoughts, at that point feeling a little depressed. Perusing through project lists on my computer, the acceptance slowly began to build, and then I had an epiphany. The new stretcher-only team would have to get a great number of projects going. Patient Handling would not make 20 percent on our existing projects.

A day earlier, the combined Medical Division was the leader in hospital stretchers and had significant growth opportunities in the specialty hospital bed markets. We had only captured a small market share in ICU beds at that time, and our budding maternity bed business had significant growth opportunities. To meet the 20-percent objective, it was clear that the bed market held our best opportunities. I had spent a great deal of time and energy to get my teams working closely with sales, marketing, and customers to define the opportunities in beds. Now everything related to beds was someone else's responsibility. My new, smaller team would have to find the growth potential in the patient-handling markets. The shift in mindset was dramatic. The most poignant thought was: *Oh my God, we have so much to do.*

Thoughts I would have never had one day before began to flood my mind. How can we improve our products in a dramatic way for the stretcher customers? What opportunities are there in specialty stretchers? Have we really delivered everything that people want in outpatient surgery platforms? What other markets might be logical offshoots for a team capable of inventing, making, and selling the best hospital stretcher products in the world? I had not previously thought about these things with the same level of intensity. Now, with the clarity of 20-percent growth being demanded in this narrowed product range, we would have to dig deeper and uncover new possibilities. This mental transformation was one of the most powerful experiences of my business career.

I met with Ken Palmer, the newly appointed general manager for

Patient Handling, at the end of that day. He had undergone the shift as well. One day he was the senior VP of operations and engineering, focusing on doing everything possible to optimize and improve our joint manufacturing and engineering efforts; the next, he was totally consumed with figuring out how to grow the stretcher business.

Ken and I had both undergone the mental transition and could only smile at the realization that this was the right way to grow a company. We felt as if we had been led down a dark and twisting path by a genius who knew the shortcut to the palace. Patient Handling would go on over the next three years to see astounding financial success and to develop great new technologies that dramatically improved the way patients are handled in the hospital and prehospital environments throughout the developed world. Without the split in 1992, few of those advancements would have happened. Simply put, our minds and energy would have been devoted elsewhere.

SIBLING RIVALRY

With the constant splitting of businesses, the centralization–decentralization debate also began to wage. Centralization advocates would be quiet for a time once a split had been declared, not wanting to appear unsupportive. But they would lie in wait to argue lost efficiencies, forgone opportunities, and unhealthy competition between the newly separated teams. Although they might find some sympathetic ears at the divisional level, from Brown's CEO seat, these arguments would fall on mostly deaf ears. Brown acknowledged the competition that arose between divisions, but instead of condemning it, he encouraged it. Stryker was like a highly competitive family of overachievers. Each sibling wanted to outdo the others, and the parents saw that as a good thing. However, if anyone from outside the family challenged one of the siblings, that challenger would incur the full force of the entire family rallying in support of their challenged sibling.

This is not to say that Brown encouraged dissension. Sibling rivalry is one thing, but actively working against each other would not be tolerated. Brown believed that competition brought out the best in people, and he stimulated healthy contests. At the same time, he also took actions to ensure that leaders and managers would learn from the successes and failures of their compatriots. Between the division presidents, there was significant collaboration and mutual respect. Each one wanted to be at the top of the performance lists, but they all knew that 20-percent growth was ultimately a total team goal.

Below the divisional presidents, Brown would become personally involved in encouraging teamwork and strong collaboration in the backdrop of two situations. First, if a division was struggling in some aspect of its performance, they would receive "help" from Corporate. Invariably this help would include handpicked experts from other divisions who were seeing success in those parts of their business. It was a great honor to be a part of these expert teams, albeit you would learn quickly that maintaining your reputation as an expert would depend on successfully improving the results of the team you were assisting. You were always held accountable; if you were there to help, there was no free pass.

Second, Brown would constantly highlight unusually successful divisions. This was a highly effective way of enticing collaboration. If a division was seen as highly successful in one area, other divisions would want to learn what their sister division was doing. Although it was also true that other divisions would often double their efforts in that area in an attempt to show up the touted expert, this led to increased performance for every part of the organization. You strove for the expert, highest-performing position.

In such an environment of competitive high achievers, the process could also become rather humbling; and ascending to the top was nearly guaranteed to be a short-term experience. Fiercely competitive, highly engaged people from other divisions were all fighting to climb higher.

By the early 1990s, the company had nine operating divisions. The corporate office housed only a tiny legal team, a two-person regulatory-affairs office, and a group of accountants under the CFO. Every other function was decentralized. Stryker took focus through decentralization to an extreme. Many companies divide into strategic business units during certain phases of their growth, but nearly all fall short of the radical decentralization seen at Stryker. The extreme separation was central to defining the purpose; the goal of 20-percent growth became ever more granular a measurement and ever more personal.

If we view the centralization–decentralization debate from Stryker Corporation's perspective during the growth years, history would side with the decentralization advocates. Through fierce competition among divisions, Stryker's structure capitalized on the benefits of the human sense of ownership and the commitment that comes from a close-knit group working together to achieve very difficult goals. The negatives of intradivisional competition were overcome by the positives of a fierce, competitive spirit and the tremendous energy the team could muster if one of the family members encountered severe issues.

DECENTRALIZATION CATALYZES GROWTH

Harry Carmitchel (one-time president of Stryker Medical) once told me about a well-known national consulting team's presentation to Brown during the late '80s or early '90s. The consultants had completed a comprehensive study for Stryker and were reviewing their findings with Brown and the corporate leadership team.

I will paraphrase the conversation: "In conclusion, Mr. Brown, you could save millions of dollars next year by some simple consolidation. Eliminate all this unnecessary duplication. You have five divisional R&D leaders; nine marketing and sales teams, each with a director/VP; eight manufacturing locations; all these divisional presidents and divisional staffs with separate human resources and accounting. Consolidate those things that don't need to be separate and greatly reduce all this divisional overhead. You could add an extra $10 million to the bottom line next year through reduction of overhead."

Brown, who was looking through the reports, pushed his reading glasses down his nose so he could look over them. We all knew that something deeply insightful or highly critical always followed this gesture. In his kind, gentlemanly Tennessee accent, he responded. "Thank you for your thorough analysis. I believe your conclusions are right. We could save $10 million next year. But . . . ," and he paused before continuing, "that would be our last year of 20-percent growth. You see, our growth is about the duplicated people. It is the investment in them, the ideas they bring to their markets, the energy they expend working to solve their customers' problems, the commitment they have to their numbers, and the high level of accountability and autonomy they feel that fuels their desire to win. This duplication creates the magic that generates our growth. I think we will just stick with the structure we have."

Focus through decentralization was a part of the culture of accountability and vice versa. All of this was about creating and evolving an organization that would achieve 20-percent growth forever. The divisional splits, the financial reviews, and the focus on the basics (*invent it, make it, sell it*) were meant to maximize the potential for high-achieving, highly responsible people to position themselves and their coworkers to deliver constant earnings growth.

9

ORGANIZING AROUND STRENGTHS AT STRYKER

Similar to Task Force 4-68, Stryker organized, structured, and even formulated its fundamental approach to key businesses around the strengths of its people. This is another example of an extreme behavior jointly exhibited by these ultrahigh-performance organizations. Stryker's leadership did not just attempt to find the correct fit for people within the existing structure; in many instances, John Brown and the divisional presidents restructured businesses and defined new jobs—even long-term plans for the company—around the individual strengths of key employees. The flexibility and constant evolution of the organizational structure were a testament to this dynamic approach.

Especially in the early years, 20-percent earnings growth went nearly hand in hand with 20-percent revenue growth. This meant that sales would double about every 3.7 years. Essentially, the size of the organization would double in that same time. The 20-percent mantra every quarter, every year did not allow anyone to pause; maintaining such growth required the people and the organization to keep up. Recruiting seldom stayed on pace with the growth, and Brown was always very concerned if headcount rose quickly. The employees were constantly stretched, and the strengths-based approach held it all together. A rising star in manufacturing might be leading a five-person cell one year and a forty-person team the next. It was a fabulous environment for performers.

In a typical Stryker career story, one intelligent, energetic young man joined the organization as an assembler for bedside rails. Very soon he demonstrated strengths in leadership and quickly became a work cell leader. He then demonstrated capability in communicating and working with suppliers to ensure his work cell had parts. He exhibited a great deal of focus and a strong desire for constant improvement. Recognizing these strengths, his division leadership made him an associate buyer, then a buyer, then a buyer/planner, then a purchasing/planning team leader, then a project leader for the most important initiative for that division's manufacturing organization, then the leader with broad responsibility for manufacturing the division's fastest-growing product line, then for the division's largest product line. Eventually, he would lead global sourcing for half the corporation—from assembler to senior director. He did this all in the span of fifteen years. Fast-paced career stories such as this were not unusual; they were widespread. With 20-percent growth, there was always more important work to be done than we had the people and time for. Those who demonstrated skill in needed areas were quickly promoted; slowing growth so the organization could catch up was unthinkable.

LAUNCHING THE EMS BUSINESS

Stryker also placed big bets on people. In 1992, the Patient Handling Division was the world leader in the hospital emergency-room stretcher market. Seeking new opportunities, the division's marketing teams investigated the prehospital (or ambulance) stretcher market. The initial conclusion was that there was little room for a new entry in the market, so they passed.

Dismayed at the current state of technology available for paramedics and Emergency Medical Technicians (EMTs), I felt the marketing team had neither looked deeply enough nor adequately considered our capability to engineer top-quality equipment. A few colleagues who agreed with me joined in, and we launched a below-the-radar, off-hours effort to develop a comprehensive business plan for entry into the EMS equipment market. We were so enthused that we considered starting it on our own if Stryker passed again.

I had only been with the company for about four years at this point and felt uncertain whether this effort would be successful or get me fired. To my delight, as the team began to reveal what we were doing, everyone up the leadership chain liked the plan. The Medical Division was busy with a massive effort to enter the general patient hospital bed market and had no spare funds to allocate to our effort, so we needed to ask Corporate for start-up type funding in the first year. This culminated in a presentation to John Brown and Dave Simpson (the CFO). At the end of the presentation, Brown removed his glasses and made two points.

First, he said, "This is the type of activity we want to have happening in all the divisions." He made it clear that entrepreneurial efforts should be applauded and thanked the team for the work they had done.

Second, he stated, "It looks like I am going to lose my old friend El Bourgraf." This told us that Brown had accepted the plan. Elroy Bourgraf was the innovative cofounder and owner of Ferno-Washington, the global leader in EMS equipment at the time; Brown had worked closely with him in his early days at Stryker attempting to link EMS cots and hospital stretchers.

We were asking for $2 million in extra funding that year, and he essentially agreed to $1 million. We were off and running.

Shortly after the presentation, I met with Harry Carmitchel (Medical Division president), who made a point of explaining the decision. In my recollection, the conversation went something like this:

"Gary," he said, "the analysis of the market you presented and the product concepts were great, but those things are not why Brown agreed. He agreed because he believed in placing a bet on you and your team."

We broke out a start-up team, including marketing, operations, and engineering. This was outside of the functional structure, which gave us the independence to pursue the EMS dream.

LEADERSHIP MATTERS TOO

Over the years, Stryker would take this strengths-based approach to far-reaching levels. In the early 1990s, resourceful human-resource leaders in the Surgical Group began working with the Gallup organization, out of Lincoln, Nebraska. This started as an investigation into personality-profiling tools to help sales managers improve hiring. Early results were positive and noticeable, and the Gallup relationship quickly evolved into a sophisticated system of statistical strength profiles based on expert interviews from Gallup analysts for positions throughout the surgical divisions. As word of their success spread, other divisions became interested in the candidate profiling, strengths-based management, team building, and leadership coaching Gallup was developing. It was just the beginning.

The partnership with Gallup fundamentally improved the recruiting process at Stryker. Nonetheless, the ability to recruit top talent was not analogous with TF 4-68. The actual results at a superhigh-performance organization such as Task Force 4-68 bring into question the notion that acquiring talent is an absolute requirement. Dibella, for the most part, had to play with the hand he was dealt. Unquestionably, talent is an important part of the equation, but it is only a part. Although Dibella may have been able to achieve even more if the Army personnel system gave him more flexibility, Stryker's flexibility did not ensure their continued success: Following Brown's retirement, the more highly talented (according to Gallup's profiles) team at Stryker has not come close to delivering a 20-percent earnings growth year in quite some time.

The profiles and selection methods greatly added to the pool of available talent. Nevertheless, it was the absolute clarity of purpose, empowered by obsession and realized by an unleashed creativity, that harnessed the capabilities of this talent pool to achieve ultrahigh levels of performance. Success is not just about the talent of a team; leadership matters!

10

STRYKER'S

UNWAVERING SUPPORT

FROM THE TOP

In July of 1976, Lee Stryker, then president of the company and son of founder Dr. Homer Stryker, perished in a tragic aviation accident while on vacation in Wyoming. Lee was piloting his own plane when all the occupants, including his wife and two companions, died in a catastrophic crash. Having lost its leader and Homer's rightful heir, Dr. Stryker and the board identified a maverick young Bristol-Myers-Squibb executive who was working as the general manager of Weck, a small medical-device subsidiary of Squibb. Members of the Upjohn family, founders of Kalamazoo-based pharmaceutical giant Upjohn, were prominent on the board and wanted to ensure Stryker hired the best person for the job. John Brown seemed to them to be the right fit, but he wasn't so sure.

"I rejected the first offer they gave me," he said. "It wasn't because it was not a good offer; it was because I was very concerned that the board was trying to replace their friend, and I knew that I could not do that. So it was an expectation that I did not feel I could live up to."

Eventually they convinced him that he was the man for the job, but he wanted to be sure of unanimous support from the board. The selection committee canvassed the board, and they were all in agreement. Brown negotiated a small 5-percent equity stake (post-IPO) in the little medical-device company from Kalamazoo, which would grow to be worth well over a billion dollars by the time he retired.

Dr. Stryker and the board had hired John Brown as president and chief executive officer. In his first years, Brown made a number of personnel moves and brought on several new people who reinvigorated the company's leadership. Although he was only beginning to prove himself, the board consistently supported his actions. His first significant acquisition brought some controversy; but again, the board's support was unwavering.

Brown recalled in our 2015 conversation, "To be fair, not a single one of the directors—and they won't remember this—not a single one agreed with the action. But the confidence they placed in me, saying 'We don't agree with you, but we'll support you,' was really meaningful. And it was typical of the relationship we developed over the years. I think that is what every CEO is longing for—to have the kind of relationship where you really can do what you think is appropriate and know that the board is not going to undercut you. And they didn't."

The board backed the initiatives Brown and the leadership team proposed, including many important acquisitions that significantly expanded the breadth and depth of the company's product lines. Over time, several members of the board became actively involved in the search for new businesses and new technologies to acquire. All of this lent even greater credence to the ubiquity of the 20-percent goal. It was clear internally and externally that the Stryker board would give Brown and his team the resources needed to continue the quest. Their actions erased any doubts regarding the support for the direction Brown was taking the company or for the high-growth requirements imposed on the divisions.

Once they had settled on the 20-percent goal, there was also significant support. As Brown told it, "There was no dissent about our 20-percent goal. I would say there was always a caution: 'John, you're setting this very high goal; make sure that your people don't do anything wrong.' So there was always a concern on the board's part—and rightfully so—that people would take a shortcut or do something illegal just to make their annual bonus or hit their goals. If we found anyone doing anything wrong—financially or legally—they were out of there. But I don't recall any director every questioning the 20 percent. To the contrary, they became some of our more enthusiastic supporters in the marketplace."

CLOSELY HELD SHARES

Stryker's ownership structure following the IPO was also helpful. After Homer's passing in 1980, Lee's three children, Rhonda, Pat, and Jon, inherited a collective ownership of the firm, totaling over 25 percent of the outstanding shares, through the family trust. John Brown maintained a 5-percent ownership in the company following the IPO. This 30-percent combined ownership gave the family and Brown a great deal of flexibility in deciding how to run the company. The family was completely supportive of what Brown was doing. As the years of 20-percent growth continued, it would have been difficult for anyone to complain about the company's management. Not seeking to cash out or sell the company, the board continued to support every initiative that would help the growth continue. Acquisitions, capital expenditures, and approval of annual plans all served to accelerate the 20-percent mindset.

When the company was still small, speculation often mounted that Stryker might be a takeover target for some large medical-device or pharmaceutical firm. But the significant percentage of the ownership by the Stryker family, John Brown, and other insiders made the likelihood of a takeover just about zero. Sometimes it was almost humorous. During the early 1990s, there was a rumor running rampant through Wall Street that medical-device giant Johnson & Johnson was considering acquiring Stryker. The endoscopy division, in particular, was in the sights because it was a leader in camera technology for endoscopic procedures, and the laparoscopic cholecystectomy (a minimally invasive surgery to remove the gall bladder) was all the craze. The lap-choly, as it was called, turned a procedure involving a main-line operating theater, extensive general anesthesia, and a three- to four-day hospital stay into an outpatient, same-day process.

Knowing the ownership structure, CFO Dave Simpson at the time talked tongue-in-cheek about a conversation with an analyst who called about the rumor: "Heck, is it Johnson & Johnson, or Howard Johnson's that you think is going to acquire us?"

Stryker would stay independent. The key shareholders were quite happy with 20-percent annual earnings growth. This near-certain independence gave the company's leaders great freedom to concentrate on what the company was doing and to think long term.

LONG-TERM APPROACH

The final source of unwavering support was the long-term shareholders themselves, the owners of the company outside of the Stryker family. John Brown took a straightforward approach to managing expectations for this group. Contrasting his approach with that common among other CEOs, Brown told me, "I am always amused when they talk about—well—our sales will be in the solid range from this number to that number, and our profit will be from this number to that number. We never did that, as you know. We always said, 'This is our sales goal; this is our profit goal,' and everybody inside knew what it was; everybody outside knew what it was. So, there was never a question about what we were going to do. I don't recall ever being criticized that we didn't meet our expectations. We think it was because we were very, very specific, we did not make any excuses, and we went for it."

He chose 20-percent earnings growth based on the belief that, over the long haul, earnings were the best and most accurate measure of enterprise performance. At shareholder or employee meetings, when he was asked about the stock price (typically when it was down), he would commonly answer, "Over the long term, a stock's price tends to follow a company's earnings. If we continue to deliver consistent 20-percent earnings growth, we believe the stock price over time will reflect our success." As analysts and investors rode waves of sentiment, the political climate changed, bear and bull market cycles repeated, and industry trends changed; Stryker Corporation relentlessly and unstoppably moved forward. In the short term, the stock price was frequently affected by exogenous events, but in the long term, it tracked the earnings growth.

Short-term investors never quite caught on to the growth process while it was occurring. It was 20 percent forever, but also 20 percent each quarter and each year. As the company consistently delivered quarter after quarter and year after year, it was interesting to watch its market valuation change. Stryker's market capitalization (stock price × number of shares outstanding) tracked earnings growth over the long term, but the short-term swings were wide. Over the years, the PE (stock price ÷ earnings per share) varied from a low of around 12 to a high of nearly 80. All the while, the company continued to deliver 20-percent EPS growth, year in and year out. As a case study, Stryker's stock performance would certainly bring into question the idea of a rational market in the short or intermediate term.

Nevertheless, for the insiders and long-term shareholders who maintained control of the company, there was never anything but support for John Brown and the 20-percent objective. Over twenty-eight years and 112 quarters, he never let them down.

PART 2

EMPOWERED OBSESSION

The clarity of purpose that John Brown and Fred Dibella trumpeted within their respective organizations made it crystal clear what the top leader was most concerned about achieving. This clarity in and of itself had a significant impact within their organizations. Nonetheless, it was not enough to achieve their stunning levels of performance. Brown and Dibella were both seriously afflicted by an absolute, monomaniacal obsession, and spreading that obsession throughout the organization—every person, process, and method of measuring anything meaningful—was central to their leadership. These leaders wanted everyone to feel the same maniacal need to achieve the goal.

Each organization reached a tipping point when achieving the purpose became deeply personal for an influential subset of their members. After this tipping point, they achieved a seemingly unstoppable momentum in the form of highly engaged teams, with an ever-increasing contingent of fanatics, all driving to deliver extraordinary results. Clarity was the foundation, but the walls and roof were built of shared obsession.

The energy was like that of a sailing ship's desperate crew on the edge of a ferocious storm. With fanatical passion, they pour every ounce of energy and strength into propelling the boat faster. Their very survival is at stake: The slightest pause and the mother of all storms will consume them. Absolute commitment and dogged determination allow them to stay just ahead of the crashing waves. Every crew member must execute their tasks with excellence and precision; and if savage swells sweep across the decks, preventing a crew member from achieving their task, the others rally even greater energy. They put aside any differences or other considerations and work together to maintain speed in the seemingly impossible situation. Through the long night and into a day that seems to last forever, these superhuman efforts allow them to navigate the tempest that would have consumed any other crew.

In most organizations, well-formed objectives are simple and straightforward, such as achieving a plan approved by a board of directors, launching critical new products on schedule, or gaining a certain amount of market share. Such goals help focus activities, and they provide a means for measurement of success. What Dibella and Brown did had an impact equal to that times ten. By empowering obsession, the singular purpose became a goal on the most powerful steroids imaginable. It was the metagoal from which every other goal sprouted.

As I look back on this process and note the similarities within the organizations, four common themes stand out.

First, these two leaders exhibited a high level of personal commitment and an extreme work ethic that inspired trust; earned respect; and, over time, gained what I can best describe as a deep reverence in the eyes of their organizations.

Second, they created stable, close-knit teams, knowing that in such high-camaraderie environments, the true power of human potential could be harnessed.

Third, they inspired an enthusiastic expectation that every team member's actions would make a difference—if not the critical difference—in achieving the purpose. What you did mattered.

Finally, they rewarded key people in a fashion that emphasized how significant an impact achieving the purpose could and would have on their lives and careers.

All of these elements empowered the organizations' members to initiate their own deeply rooted, personal motivation to achieve the purpose. Once this internalization became pervasive, the organization reached that tipping point, and the human energy spread like wildfire. The passion developed in these two organizations was not normal; it was extreme. It was over the top. It was radical. It was even borderline pathological. In an assumed backdrop of personal integrity and honesty, there was nothing more important than achieving the purpose. Nothing.

11

BUILDING TRUST

AND EARNING RESPECT

IN 4-68 ARMOR

Fred Dibella took command of 4-68 shortly after I arrived at Fort Carson. I was an inexperienced second lieutenant, recently out of West Point and the Armor Basic Officer Leaders Course. I remember some of the senior sergeants expressing skepticism whether this new commander, a United States Military Academy graduate with a background as an attack helicopter pilot, would be any better than the last commander. During Dibella's change-of-command ceremony, he introduced himself to the battalion. In his folksy, Southern Illinois accent, he discussed things he liked and things he did not like. He added a bit of humor and generally came off as a genuine person interested in establishing a rapport with the troops and setting some goals for the battalion. He mentioned that he liked winning and hated losing, but at the time, none of us knew the extremes of those preferences.

Sometimes much can be revealed about the character of a leader by considering whom they admire among the great leaders of the past. Dibella's heroes were unique individuals who had demonstrated excellence in leading soldiers in battle. Noted Civil War historian and author Michael Shaara wrote a moving tale of the Battle of Gettysburg in his book *The Killer Angels*, which became a hit movie in 1993. The book moved Dibella so much that he made it mandatory reading for every officer in the battalion.

Dibella revered Joshua Lawrence Chamberlain, a college professor from Maine who led troops in the Union Army during the Civil War. Colonel Chamberlain's 20th Maine regiment was the unit that, on the second major day of battle at Gettysburg, miraculously held the Union's left flank on Little Round Top, despite multiple Confederate assaults. Under each assault, the valiant Union defense held, even if only by the narrowest of margins. Chamberlain, exhausted late in the day, could see the Rebels massing for a final attack. Outnumbered and nearly out of ammunition, he knew his regiment would not stand in the face of the Confederate's impending push up the hill. Losing the Union's flank could result in a loss of the entire battle, because the Confederates could press the Union off the high ground.

In desperation, Chamberlain ordered his troops to fix bayonets and charge into the assaulting Confederate troops. The Confederates were taken by surprise and stunned at the ferocity of a Union charge. The Southern soldiers' morale disintegrated, and the former attackers retreated or surrendered en masse. The Union flank held.

The next day, Robert E. Lee would lose many of his most valuable troops in an ill-fated charge into the center of the Union position—a flawed plan that was partially motivated by the belief that the Union flanks were too strong to overcome.

Dibella would quote Chamberlin by saying, "Two things an officer must do to lead men: You must show physical courage, and you must care for their welfare."

To Fred Dibella, this meant that effective officers would lead by example and would work with all diligence to take care of their soldiers. It was incumbent on leaders to be physically fit and technically and tactically proficient. To gain the trust and respect of the men, leaders had to show personal courage. He took the opportunity to do this from the start.

DEMONSTRATING PERSONAL COURAGE

When Dibella assumed command of 4-68, the battalion was performing its annual Tank Table 8 (TT8) gunnery exercise. This was a field-training qualification drill in which each individual tank crew would travel along a firing range while being presented with targets, which the tank would need to properly engage and destroy using live ammunition. It was an annual rite of passage for a tank crew and one treated with a great deal of seriousness. Crews would receive a score for their proficiency in spotting targets, effective maneuvering, fire command accuracy, and gunnery accuracy (hitting the targets). The scale was up to 1,000 points, and you had to hit 700 to have a passing score. The top-scoring crews would gain bragging rights for the next year.

A tank battalion commander, according to the Table of Organization and Equipment (TO&E), is also the commander of their own tank with its four-person crew. The commander was officially expected to participate annually in the TT8 qualifications, even though many did not; Dibella's predecessor had not made a single run on TT8. With only hours to train, no one expected that our new battalion commander would take part in the gunnery exercise, especially given his background as an aviator. Dibella saw this as an opportunity to demonstrate courage and earn a level of trust with the troops.

He had been in a Pentagon desk job for the previous two years, and out of contact with tanks for much longer. However, he knew the commander of Bravo Company, Joe Moore. Dibella had been the tactical officer overseeing Moore's cadet company at West Point. He called Moore and asked him to select a crack crew ready for TT8.

Even with a highly talented crew, the tank commander has a great impact on the crew's score for gunnery exercises. He must get the fire commands exactly right. He must sight the targets and slew the main gun to the general location of the target before handing the controls over to the gunner. Dibella rehearsed the fire commands with his son hundreds and hundreds of times on their road trip from Washington, DC, to Fort Carson. Dibella knew that effectively leading these troops, whose confidence had been shaken by their previous commander, would require a demonstration of physical courage. Qualifying on TT8 when most expected he would not even participate would go a long way to earning that confidence. As it turned out, he not only qualified, but he and his crew racked up a perfect score—the highest in the battalion.

Building on the TT8 reputation, 4-68's first major exercise under Dibella's command took place at a new training area in southern Colorado called Piñon Canyon. Headquarters likely wanted to ensure the fiery young lieutenant colonel received an appropriate welcome to the challenges of leading a battalion in the field. Although the outcomes were nowhere close to what 4-68 would encounter in later rotations, the impact Dibella made during this first training exercise was striking.

My platoon was cross-attached to another unit at the time and did not attend the training exercise, so I could watch the early evolutions of 4-68's transformation from a figurative distance. It was fascinating to witness the growing engagement of the 4-68 leadership, especially below the company-commander level. When I talked with 4-68's NCOs and junior officers after that first exercise, they were almost giddy with enthusiasm.

To paraphrase how some of the senior sergeants described a key incident, "The entire task force was engaged in a Multiple Integrated Laser Engagement System (MILES)-simulated battle exercise against a company from another task force. We were conducting a sunrise attack, and we were starting to have success driving into the flank of the enemy. 4-68's battle plan involved using smoke set between the enemy front line and the 4-68 tank company maneuvering to the enemy flank, to obscure this decisive movement from the enemy. It was working beautifully, but one of the staff officers in the brigade (higher headquarters) observing the operation must have thought the smoke screen was somehow inappropriate or unrealistic. The observer came on the battalion command net (a radio frequency to which each company commander and the battalion HQ were connected) and demanded that the smoke screen be halted.

"We all knew that this was the end of our smoke screen, except that it wasn't. Dibella went off. He screamed back at the observer in earshot of everyone on the battalion command net, saying that the screen was legitimate and told his commanders that under no circumstances were they to halt the smoke generators. The incident sharpened the nerves of everyone in the battalion. Bravo Company completed the flanking move under cover of the smoke, and we totally destroyed the enemy units on the objective."

It was unheard of that a maneuver unit commander would challenge a brigade observer. Stories of this interchange between brigade and the bold new task-force commander spread like wildfire throughout the battalion.

One of the respected senior sergeants who was skeptical of all new commanders responded like this: "We got ourselves a colonel!"

This incident and several similar ones ignited the trust between the soldiers and their commander. The leaders were also beginning to believe that LTC Dibella was someone who would stand up for us and allow creativity and innovation. Dibella made it clear that he was out to win the simulations and that he would support his troops.

The smoke screen incident and TT8 were just two of many small things that served to build an environment of trust in the unit. After every field exercise, the battalion conducted After-Action Reviews

(AARs). Sometimes only Dibella, the five company commanders, and the battalion executive officer would attend these sessions. However, if time permitted, Dibella would include every officer. This inclusiveness served to further the feeling of trust throughout the unit. Junior officers knew what was being discussed and what was not being discussed about their crucial field performance. Dibella and others used the forum to personally call out individuals for exceptional actions. It was an environment where we could also be brutally honest about things individual units or officers could have done better.

This level of openness in communication was monumental for the 1980s military. At that time, military officers' careers could be made or broken by one missed check mark in a senior rater's ranking of an Officer Efficiency Report. Dibella's colloquial style helped ease the tension in the reviews. He cracked jokes about failed actions, and it was clear that the intent was to inspire and teach. Through review after review, ego defenses declined, trust increased, and learning from each exercise improved. As we slowly made fewer mistakes and began to win more and more, the effect was contagious.

A former captain on the S3 (operations team) recalled, "Everybody had input, and we were continuously reevaluating, tweaking here and there. It was a great creative process. You could see everybody that had a piece to play becoming masters of their craft in their particular areas."

Trust was developing up and down the organization that the purpose—defeating OPFOR 9–0—was the top priority, not just words. The task force was learning that if you were doing all you could to win, the leadership would have your back; and if some people, particularly those in leadership positions, were not able to catch on, they would not be allowed to bring the entire unit down.

For example, one platoon leader continually demonstrated his inability to effectively lead his platoon in the simulated battles. Company commanders and experienced platoon leaders knew he was struggling and showing no signs of improvement or even motivation to do so. In peacetime, this problem would persist 99 times out of 100, and the task force would simply have to find some way to work with the weakness of one platoon, so there was little expectation that anything would change. The situation was complicated by the fact that this lieutenant's father was a general. But if one of only six tank platoons was weak, the purpose was in serious jeopardy.

Dibella and the man's frontline commander had started the process of documenting the issues with the young officer, but it would typically take a series of horrible reports, multiple counseling sessions, and attempts at rehabilitation or remediation before a change could be made. Dibella had earned enough trust in the NCO ranks at this point that three sergeants from the lieutenant's platoon had the courage to make an appeal to him.

"Sir," they said, "we have bought into the goal of this task force: We want to contribute to an undefeated NTC rotation. But we cannot get there with this lieutenant. We have tried for six months now, but he does not know what he's doing, he cannot or will not learn or improve, and he's gonna lead us to disaster."

The appeal resonated with Chamberlain's two things that an officer must do—demonstrate courage and care for their soldiers' welfare—so Dibella felt compelled to act.

Later, he would recall the situation: "Some things can be seen as clear as God's blue sky, if you have the vision. This young man belonged in a civilian accounting office; he was miserable as a combat officer. So I called Colonel Davis on the secure FM radio on the way to the lieutenant's location and gave him my intentions, in blunt but respectful terms. Davis was a man of few words. I believe he responded with something like, 'We may be kicking a hornet's nest, but carry on.' So I did. I took the lieutenant away from his unit in my jeep, and I personally drove him to a secluded location. That's where I relieved him, and I tried very hard to do it right.

"See, this was not a bad kid. He was just in a horribly wrong place.

He was miserable, and my soldiers under his command were even more miserable. I told him that I honestly believed this was a good thing for him, that he had to understand that this was a watershed event in his life. It was an opportunity to head in a better direction, a direction more suited to his skills and his heart, before he did serious damage to his soldiers and his unit.

"I cannot honestly say whether he was comforted or concerned, thankful or embarrassed. He was tough to read. But he carried on."

Dibella continued, "I had his platoon sergeant gather his belongings, and I drove him back to task force HQ, where my sergeant major took him back to the main post area. Meanwhile, I went back to his platoon, and I explained everything to his sergeants and soldiers, including the fact that some men are just not cut out to bear the enormous burden of leading American soldiers, and that the soldiers in 4-68 deserved nothing less than the best I could give them. In all my years in uniform, I never saw such gratitude and respect in the eyes of twenty men. It was a good day.

"Major General Bartlett called the man's father. He ran that inter-ference for me, and it was probably a good thing."

For the most part Dibella had to play with the cards he was dealt from a personnel standpoint, but in this critical instance, he exhibited the courage and initiative to gain at least one new card. The action also demonstrated to the officers and NCOs that Fred Dibella would stick out his own neck to do what was necessary to give the task force every chance at winning.

Some might think that this action would inspire fear in the hearts of other platoon leaders, but it was quite the opposite. Following the field exercise, Dave Carruthers (my company commander) gathered all the lieutenants into his office to explain the situation. He made sure that I made it to the meeting, even though my platoon was still cross-attached to the other task force.

He said something along the lines of "None of you have anything to worry about; you all get it. I have confidence in every one of you. Your soldiers have confidence in you. This is a good thing; this lieutenant did not belong leading one of the task force's platoons. A lot of people tried to work with him, but it was going nowhere."

We all recognized it as the right move to make. And we knew from that moment that if we were working in the best interests of the task force, the colonel had our backs.

PERSONAL INTEGRITY IN 4-68

Dibella made it clear that personal integrity was tantamount and that lying, cheating, and stealing were not tolerated at any level. He was absolutely driven to win, but it had to be a clean win. He developed this ethos in an empowering way.

Describing it years later, he would recall, "One of the most crucial aspects of the whole process was the information we needed from the scout platoon, from Charlie Mech when they were in the forward defense position, and from Team Bravo when they were leading in the movement to contact. We made an intentionally dramatic—overly dramatic—point of what happens when wrong information is transmitted. There are a lot of incentives to transmit wrong information. For example, if Ramsgard (the scout platoon leader) is supposed to have crossed the LD (Line of Departure) at 0300, and his platoon is a little bit late and he did not cross until 0320, but he called in at 0300, what would happen if that lie, that bit of misinformation, were actually transmitted in a combat zone? We'd create scenarios on what might have been as a result of that misinformation or that bad spot report that was intentionally misrepresented because you weren't in the position you knew you were supposed to be in. In the largest sense of that example, we tried early on to make certain that everybody had the confidence to make mistakes knowing full well that they would not be destroyed or reprimanded for that. Call in and say you're twenty minutes late on the

LD. You're still my scout platoon leader. You're still Rambo Ramsgard. You're still the best I've got. I still love you like a son. Just call it accurately, and don't ever deceive anyone at anytime. Don't ever intentionally distort the truth."

The NCOs and officers were beginning to see that this lieutenant colonel was something special. He would choose the more difficult path. He would do what had the greatest likelihood of improving the combat effectiveness of the unit, whether that would be favorably viewed from the outside or not. He would take personal and career risks for the betterment of the unit. You could trust him, and this trust was the foundation of the deep respect that grew over time. Through this earned trust, Dibella engaged a part of the human spirit that exists only at some fundamental mammalian level. It was not a part of our higher brain; it was primordial, irrational, and powerful. Like a highly lethal wolf pack that follows its alpha leader, we followed Dibella.

12

CREATING STABLE, CLOSE-KNIT TEAMS IN 4-68

Dibella studied the research regarding soldiers' motivation to risk their lives in combat. As he would explain it, "Men join the Army for a variety of reasons. They join for economic reasons, for patriotic reasons, for the chance to travel the world, et cetera, et cetera. And that's all fine.

"But that's not the reason men fight. Men don't fight for motherhood or apple pie. They don't fight for the Army College Fund. Men fight for one reason alone. I am not talking about a fight to survive; anybody will fight to survive. I am talking about fighting to win. Men fight *for each other*. They fight because they've grown to know each other, then trust each other, then love each other. They fight so that they don't let each other down."

STABILITY IS CRUCIAL

Another of the three pieces of mandatory reading Dibella had for officers in the task force was a document called *The Reasons Why*, a collection of notes, readings, and letters put together by Herbert J. Lloyd from the National War College. One chapter that he often quoted was "Comradeship," by Leslie D. Weatherhead.

"When a soldier was injured and could not get back to safety," Dibella recounted, "his buddy went out to get him against his officer's orders. The man returned mortally wounded and his friend, who he had carried back, was dead.

"The officer was angry. 'I told you not to go,' he said. 'Now I have lost both of you. It was not worth it.'

"The dying man replied, 'But it was. When I got to him, he said, "Jim, I knew you'd come."'"

For Fred Dibella, the moral of the story was that to build that kind of cohesion, you have to stabilize your soldiers. He would further explain it later: "As any good combat arms officer knows, the bond that is created among men through constant association is an irreplaceable advantage. We did the same thing at the task force, team, and combat-support attachment levels. We tried to keep men together."

The quasi stability TF 4-68 gained in the preparation period leading up to the rotation was an absolutely critical factor in this process. To fully understand this, it is important to realize that the prevailing methodology during this time (and which continues for many Army units today) was to put together a customized combined arms task force based on the next day's impending mission requirements and troop availability. Brigade-level commanders would arrange their units for the operations by task, organizing into battalion-level task forces that could include any combination of the brigade's tank and mechanized infantry companies, depending on the needs of the mission. Support and service-support units from within the brigade and division would be similarly grouped together for an operation and then reassigned according to the next mission. The impetus for this structure was flexibility and custom makeup of the combat power for the task at hand. Commanders of an armor battalion might one day find themselves with a mission that would be suited for a pure tank (four-tank company) operation and the very next day change to a mission having three mech companies and only one tank company.

Dibella and the Second Brigade leadership blew up that model. Colonel Davis and his battalion commanders decided that gains from stability—mainly unit-to-unit and soldier-to-soldier relationships—would trump any gains that might come from tailoring the organization for a particular mission.

As Dibella put it in a later presentation, "Task organize to keep men together so they grow to know each other, trust each other, and love each other, and they won't let each other down. Train them to a razor's edge, bond them together, and treat them like pieces of gold."

Second Brigade went to great lengths to keep the organization constant in field operations and in all other activities, including garrison (when the units were at home on the Army base).

The brigade accepted the trade-offs such a devotion to stability would have. Battalion motor pool facilities for a tank battalion were quite different from those for a mechanized infantry battalion. Nonetheless, Colonel Davis put the mech companies into the tank battalion motor pools and other spaces in garrison and forced his staff to figure out the systems and processes. Stability and unit cohesion for effectiveness in combat trumped every other consideration.

Dibella often spoke of Captain Peter J. Schifferle's 1985 *Armor* magazine article, "The Technology of Teamwork," which covered highly effective tank crews at the National Training Center and analyzed their common elements. Captain Schifferle found that the most telling characteristic of these crews was the length of time they were together. Crew stability was more important than any other element—IQ, time in service, past records, test scores, and so on—by a factor of four to one.

A highly lethal main battle tank requires four soldiers working together in lockstep. The actions of every crew member have to be optimally synchronized. Having a star gunner who is being jerked around by a driver that is moving at the wrong time or not maneuvering to the best firing position compromises the crew's effectiveness. Working with the same crew allows them to better synchronize over multiple missions.

I should note that stability in the Army personnel system at the time was quite different from most civilian businesses; achieving any level of consistency was highly challenging. Two- to four-year enlistments for a large percentage of soldiers meant that turnover was constant. The Army personnel system encouraged a separate developmental pathway for every soldier. With soldiers constantly transferring in and out of units, changing locations, attending training courses, and so on, a tank crew that stayed together for a month would have about average stability. Six months for a four-person crew would be extreme. A year was very rare.

As Dibella explained it, stability was step one: "If you don't stabilize, you have no chance to build a team. If you stabilize, it gives you the chance."

Empowering obsession throughout the task force could only be done with a group of men that were going to still be together nine to twelve months later, when they reached the NTC rotation. Once he gained a reasonable level of stability, he could begin building the team and spreading the maniacal desire to defeat the OPFOR as a proactive, concerted, intense effort aimed at every level of the unit. But only with unit and personnel stability would building trust and demonstrating personal commitment to the purpose have a lasting effect.

The Army also saw cross-training between soldiers as a significant initiative. Although 4-68 did the minimum required by regulations, the commanders made every effort to stabilize each individual soldier's responsibilities in the months leading up to the NTC rotation. This was another element in driving clarity at every level. Rather than have small units extensively cross-train in an attempt to become proficient at twenty different potential small-unit missions, each unit concentrated on the two or three types of missions it would be called to do based on the playbook and that unit's place in the battalion's overall operational concept.

STABILITY IN THE SUPPORTING UNITS

Dibella fought hard to gain similar levels of stability for all elements of the combined arms task force. A wide array of support units are typically attached to a battalion-level task force according to its mission. These assets are essential to effective combat, but they come with allegiance to a leadership structure from the specialty unit to which they directly report. For a combined arms force such as 4-68, these would include: engineers; nuclear, biological, and chemical support; field artillery fire support; air defense artillery; smoke; Army Aviation and Air Force liaisons; maintenance support; and others. This situation could create divided loyalties for the attached units that were not necessarily conducive to cohesion at the task-force level.

For example, the air-defense artillery attachment to TF 4-68 was part of a parent air-defense artillery battalion. That battalion's commander was responsible for effective air defense for the entire division, of which TF 4-68 was only a part. The highest-level air-defense commander in the division was responsible for training and maximizing the effectiveness of his units for the division's air-defense task. Although part of that commander's task was to send out his units into the maneuver battalions in a support role, specialized training in the nuances of air defense might be best accomplished when the air-defense units trained together. The air-defense commander might demand that certain units rotate through his training schedule at certain times. That schedule could conflict with the supported maneuver task force's schedule. According to the Army's command structure, the air-defense commander would make the final call to resolve such conflicts. That is, unless the division's commander had other ideas.

Again, to build the teamwork at the small-unit level and empower the obsession to win throughout these support units, Dibella felt stability was absolutely essential. He first worked with his peer commanders to ensure they understood his emphasis on consistency, asking that the same platoon be attached to TF 4-68 for all our training exercises. Only by working with the same platoon with the same platoon leader and platoon sergeant for every joint mission could we build the desired unit cohesion. Although this may sound trivial, it was no small task. The supporting unit's headquarters would have to make many alterations to their training schedules and other activities to allow the same subunit to always match 4-68's busy training and field exercise schedule. On many occasions, they would have to put their parent unit's schedule in a subordinate role.

Inevitably conflicts arose, but Dibella would not relent. Winning every battle at NTC would require the utmost in solidarity and team stability. The support units had to share the obsession too. Dibella played the division commander card when he needed to, and General Bartlett backed up the commanders who were bold enough to ask for assistance in reaching the goal. From the division commander's view, it was the maneuver units that were most accountable to the mission of total success at NTC. Again, this support from the top for TF 4-68's decentralized structure was a critical factor in its success. In divisions with more centralized control of support assets, maneuver task forces would not enjoy the opportunities that TF 4-68 had to build maximal cohesion for the soldiers who would fight together.

FORMING CLOSE-KNIT TEAMS

Stability formed the foundation for cohesiveness. It gave us the time to form deep bonds between soldiers at the small-unit level. This close knitting of our combat teams was another absolutely critical element in our success. The power is difficult to describe.

The 2014 movie *Fury* accurately portrays the close bond that develops within stabilized tank crews. In the movie, a diverse crew of an outgunned WWII Sherman tank is filled with clashing personalities, yet they bond together and will do anything for each other in combat. At the beginning of the movie, veteran crew members struggle to accept newbie Norman, a replacement for their fallen assistant driver. As Norman slowly finds his place with the crew, shared hardships coupled with a respect for their veteran tank commander, played by Brad Pitt, bond the crew together. Director David Ayer portrays it correctly in the movie. Norman starts as a pacifist, unwilling to fire his hull-mounted machine gun. As the crew shares the hardships of war, bonds develop. Norman begins to fight with fury not because of God and country, but because of the brotherhood he develops with the crew and their respected commander.

The movie also depicts the claustrophobic environment a crew experiences in a tank. Surrounded by tons of metal, with the constant resonance of the engine, the intermittent whir of the hydraulic system charging, the squeal of the turret motor as it turns, the rhythm of machine guns firing, the thunderous boom and vacuum-creating percussion of the main gun, the gunpowder fumes from expended machine-gun shells, and the acrid smoke from main-gun casings are all background to the private circle of communication on the vehicle's intercom and the intense brotherhood required to survive the brutal violence of combat.

Knowing you are the target for just about every advanced weapon system on the battlefield creates a special intensity for a tank crew. Highly effective tank crews are highly interdependent, and this is something that takes time to create within the team.

You have two primary roles as a tank platoon leader. First, you lead the platoon. Sixteen men and a few million dollars of sophisticated equipment are your primary focus. Second, you command one of the four tanks.

I experienced the benefits of stability and the downsides of instability firsthand with my tank crews in the two NTC rotations. Although the platoon as a whole had a stable makeup of tank commanders going through the rotations and the intensive training periods leading to each, my personal tank crew changed significantly. As you'll remember, for the first rotation the platoon was cross-attached to a different tank task force to fill out its ranks. By the time we traveled to NTC, the platoon had been together about four months. Even though this is a relatively short period, at the end of that experience I felt the team had very much come together, benefiting from the personnel stability during our intense training. We were combat ready by the end of that first rotation, but I still had much to learn as a platoon leader in a task force looking to win every battle at NTC.

The crew in that first rotation was composed of three tankers who were close friends, and it did not take long for me to find my place in that team as the tank commander. The camaraderie and bonds of stability were already there, and they accepted their young lieutenant as someone who needed to learn a great deal but cared about their welfare, seemed to be able to handle the platoon in simulated combat, and was willing to listen. Very early on we qualified with high marks on Tank Table 8 and were one of the most lethal crews of that other task force, even though the platoon was just an attachment.

Following our return, however, two members of the crew moved on to other assignments. The subsequent changes in my personal tank crew were quite disruptive. Two of four members were new and the other changed position in the tank. Moreover, these new crew members were not naturally buddies. Through the many training exercises leading to NTC, we eventually came together, and I would say we were a solid crew when we left for the rotation. By the end of the second rotation, that crew was performing like combat-hardened veterans. The stability worked its magic. We enjoyed another three months together, and I shot my best scores in gunnery exercises during that time.

By contrast, the rest of my platoon experienced the huge benefits from the stability Dibella and Second Brigade had worked so hard to maintain. The tank commanders, platoon sergeant, and almost all of the crews stayed together. By the end of this period, we were probably one of the best-prepared small units in the Army.

A STABLE PLATOON AT THE PINNACLE

Two months following our victories at NTC, Alpha Company was tasked to go to the Piñon Canyon training area and act as the OPFOR for a brigade that was preparing for their rotation. My platoon was at the pinnacle of their combat readiness.

For one particular exercise, our entire company of fourteen tanks was supposed to act as the defenders against the other task force (our attackers would have forty tank-killing systems). However, logistical issues resulted in a limited supply of the company's MILES equipment; after digging all of the company's defensive positions, we only had a platoon's worth of MILES systems.

Company commander Dave Carruthers, confident in our capabilities, said, "We are going to give the MILES to First Platoon. You go and defend the company position; we'll go find the other systems and come in as a reserve once we've installed them."

I went to the platoon and explained the situation. There were many somber faces. We were a unit used to victory, and this seemed an unwinnable scenario. But instead of lamenting our desperate situation, the platoon rallied. Many of us had seen small numbers of OPFOR vehicles take out an entire task force in that first rotation. Now it was our turn.

As our four tanks rolled off to the forward-most decoy position, we were confident in our plan, confident in each other, and ready to fight. Our plan was to fall back from the decoy positions into the first set of platoon dug-in positions once we detected enemy movement. At first we would fight from there. However, if the enemy's dismounted infantry approached the first position, we would fall back in groups of two to the next set of prepared positions—the ones that had been dug out for our sister platoons.

Two tanks would provide overwatch while the other two tanks fell back. Just before falling back, I would call for artillery barrages, and we would use onboard smoke to obscure our movements. There were three sets of platoon positions to fight from, and we hoped that, by the time we reached the final set, the rest of Alpha would come to our rescue with a counterattack. Everyone knew the plan (it was a veteran platoon from the 9–0 Silver Lion NTC rotation), but we were outnumbered ten to one in tank-killing systems, and twenty to one in soldiers.

The battle went like clockwork. We caught the attacking task force off guard, expecting us to be in the decoy positions. When they realized their intelligence was flawed, they became confused. As they regrouped, they essentially changed from a deliberate attack into a movement to contact. This was exactly what we wanted. In the span of about ten minutes, as they began moving toward our initial defensive positions, we took out most of the lead company's tanks and several of the armored personnel carriers. We encountered no casualties of our own from the well-protected dugout firing positions. Sergeant Rodriguez, my platoon sergeant, radioed that he saw some personnel carriers off to his flank that had dismounted their infantry. That was our cue. Calling for artillery on the dismounted infantry location, we fell back two at a time to the next position.

The attackers saw some movement and maneuvered a few tanks into firing positions. Unfortunately for them, our overwatch tanks took them out. The dismounted infantry was in disarray under the artillery barrage right on their position. Under the cover of smoke, we reached the second set of fighting positions. My crew was energized and executing with uncanny precision. The loader spotted the second company of attacking tanks attempting to flank opposite from the side where the dismounted infantry was being barraged by artillery. From this second set of positions, all four of my tanks could see the attackers; they were like ducks in a row. We had trained for this and knew how to distribute our fire. Each tank commander targeted a different vehicle in the enemy formation so our shots were not redundant.

All four tanks fired fanatically on the exposed attackers. Hoffman devices (to simulate the main-gun blasts) went off constantly. My tank commanders hopped out of their cupolas in a frenzy to reload the Hoffman, which you had to do according to the rules of the MILES engagement so the enemy could see a signature when your gun fired in the simulated mode. We maneuvered back and forth in the fighting positions to ensure we were only exposed when a simulated round was in the chamber, the Hoffman loaded, and our tank ready to fire.

Quite frankly, it was a turkey shoot. Twenty minutes later, all of the attacking tanks were killed, most of the opposing personnel carriers had MILES kill lights blinking, and the attacking commander had called off the assault. We heard from Carruthers on the radio a few minutes later: "Keep holding them off; we are on our way."

But there was no need.

This platoon had been together for over a year, through two NTC rotations, numerous exercises at Piñon Canyon, and countless exercises on the Fort Carson training areas. We knew each other, respected each other, and were a highly effective, highly lethal combat force. When faced with daunting odds, the platoon did the job we had trained to do, and the results were remarkable. I have rarely seen every action of an exercise executed with such near perfection. More than 90 percent of the opposing task force was destroyed, and we took no casualties.

Through the yearlong lead-up to the NTC, in a similar fashion 4-68's stabilized task force of soldiers became a highly functional collection of close-knit teams. Dibella combined all the essential human elements in empowering the obsession to win. The veteran soldiers and more senior NCOs felt that this task force and its commander were different. The stability resulting from the consistent structure and all the other elements to keep the men together had a clear impact. When the constantly revolving door of the Army personnel system stopped turning, the results were significant. We experienced the genuine advantages of this stability at all levels, but perhaps most noticeably at the small-unit level—the tank crews and infantry squads. It enabled those teams to get to know each other, care for each other, and come together to reach this insane goal of winning every battle at the NTC.

13

ACTIONS MAKING A

DIFFERENCE IN 4-68

Empowering an obsession to win also requires building a positive expectancy inside the organization. Over the long term, people and organizations tend to achieve what is within their comfort zone. That zone has both an upper and a lower bound. For example, elite runners capable of running four-minute miles in their prime years will subconsciously define their comfort zone around the 4:00 minute mark, plus or minus—say—ten seconds. If the runner performs in that zone, they will likely keep training at the current level. If they perform below the zone, their inner belief system will cause them to alter their training, practice harder, improve their diet, or work on starting techniques. They will do everything in their power to get back to their comfort zone. Likewise if they perform beyond the zone, (say 3:45), their most likely reaction would be to become complacent. They might not push the next training runs so hard.

Dibella took the worst-performing battalion in the division and turned them into winners. Task Force 4-68 radically altered its collective comfort zone without becoming overconfident. The inner belief system of the leaders and NCOs transformed from a confidence-lacking sense of despair to a genuine belief that we could defeat the highly vaunted OPFOR. Critical to this transformation was intensifying the concept of winning.

As Dibella explained, "Winning is not all-important; it is the only thing that is important. Yes, you do it by the rules, but you have to win. At the NTC, we have the most incredible training facility in the history of the planet. You can't win at the NTC unless all seven of your operating systems are working. If you don't have them all working, you are going to get your ass kicked. The OPFOR will find out which one is wrong, and they will find your weakness, and they'll punish you."

The message was simple: Every process matters. Every soldier matters. We will work together in lockstep, and we will win. Over the many field exercises leading to the NTC rotation, the unit developed a sense of confidence. As we improved our expertise in execution and further refined the battle plans from the playbook, success built on success. We won a battle, then we won the next battle. We went to Fort Irwin with great respect and admiration for the OPFOR but also with a positive expectancy: Perhaps they could be beaten. Our comfort zone had radically moved to the side of winning.

When I asked Joe Moore if he bought into the 9–0 idea at the time Dibella presented it in the auditorium, his answer was quick and unemotional. "No."

He went on to explain, "I was an NTC veteran, and I knew the reputation of the OPFOR. Beating them in every battle? I just did not believe it was possible. The odds were so stacked against the US units. I thought we could have a good rotation, but every battle?"

Keeping his skepticism to himself, Moore was maniacal about his company's combat effectiveness and tactical proficiency. Even though he and other NTC veterans were uncertain about the possibility of winning every single battle, they were totally committed to giving the OPFOR the fight of their lives. Our significant wins in the Piñon Canyon exercises prior to NTC built his confidence, but a waning skepticism still reigned in these veterans' rational minds. Nonetheless, in their hearts they felt the same positive expectancy we all did. If any unit could do it, we could.

The first battle at NTC converted Joe Moore. "We beat them handily. I mean, we destroyed them. I started to feel that we actually could do it. We were just possibly that good."

THE FIRST NTC BATTLE

After pulling out of the desert motor pool for a night march of some twenty-five kilometers into Fort Irwin's training area, we prepared for our initial battle the next day. Sphincters throughout the task force were tight in anticipation of that first contact. We moved out of the assembly area before first light. The Observer–Controllers designed this first encounter with the OPFOR as a movement to contact, with the potential of being followed by a deliberate attack toward a final objective later in the day. Our scout platoon had acquired valuable information about the enemy locations, and we had a fairly good idea where we would expect to encounter the first resistance. Everything was going as per the playbook.

Bravo Company encountered the enemy first. The scout's information was right on, and Bravo eliminated this small enemy reconnaissance element.

We then started movement toward what we expected could be the main OPFOR defensive position. On the way, the task force was only momentarily slowed while navigating through a minefield the OPFOR had erected along our route. Fortunately, Delta Force had spotted it during a night patrol and was already either clearing it or finding routes around. The smoke platoon was brilliantly laying out a thick cloud that obscured our movements from the enemy. Bravo Company and Charlie Mech went through the cleared minefield to the left. Alpha followed a route around the mines to the right, through the thick haze of smoke.

Bravo and Charlie made contact with the enemy. They were in one of the locations we suspected. Alpha Company motored through the minefield bypass into an overwatch position. Bravo and Charlie Mech maneuvered farther left to hit the OPFOR's flank. The OPFOR was caught in a deadly vise between the guns of Alpha in overwatch position and the left hook flanking maneuver from Bravo and Charlie. After a few minutes, MILES lights throughout the enemy forces lit up, indicating they were killed. The task force continued its march.

We encountered resistance by several scattered and seemingly disorganized OPFOR units on the way to the final objective. Although they were larger in number than those at the interim objective, we destroyed these other forces piecemeal and in short order before finishing our operation with clear control of the final objective.

Later, in the After-Action Review (AAR), we learned that we had gotten much farther than anyone expected. No unit had ever made it past their interim objective in the first movement to contact. The OPFOR units at the final objective were disorganized and surprised because they expected to be the defenders for the next day's deliberate attack.

After that success, even Joe Moore believed a 9–0 victory might just be possible. The last few NTC veterans, hardened by previous defeats at the hands of the OPFOR, now doubted the OPFOR's seeming invincibility. This shift of expectations would pay dividends in the battles to come. We had defeated the indomitable OPFOR and had done it decisively. Eight more battles lay ahead, and we had just notified the OPFOR command that TF 4-68 was something special. They would make significant adjustments in the battles ahead. Nonetheless, the last doubters were converting. We could actually do it!

OPEN AND HONEST COMMUNICATION

This growing expectation of success further individualized the feeling that what you did, what your crew or squad did, and what your platoon or company did could be the determining factor in the next battle. All through the exhaustive training and preparation process leading up to the NTC, the AAR process also contributed significantly to our understanding that actions mattered. These reviews were honest and open conversations about what happened in the just-finished simulated battle. When held at the task-force level, no one wanted to be the leader of a platoon or company that made mistakes, but making mistakes was all part of the process. The errors were never covered up, and there was little holding back for fear of offending someone. At the task-force level, communication was direct and, if necessary, brutally honest, but it was also safe to discuss problems and admit errors. No one was ever perfect, and no one was ever condemned for an error. This approach trickled down to the companies and platoons.

In one exercise, things went horribly wrong with Alpha Company's overwatch during a deliberate attack. We talked about it openly later. In these Piñon Canyon engagements, a Fort Carson–based unit would act as the OPFOR. Unlike at the NTC, the Fort Carson OPFOR vehicles were not made to look like Soviet forces; they looked exactly like our friendly tanks. In this simulated battle, Alpha did not correctly discern the friendly tanks from the enemy tanks and took out several of Bravo Company's vehicles with friendly fire.

Dibella and other 4-68 officers communicated in a very direct fashion during the AAR. My platoon was the worst offender in shooting the friendly tanks. I felt personally devastated and completely humiliated. Fred Dibella and Joe Moore were not interested in blaming Alpha or me; they wanted to figure out how the task force could minimize future errors of this sort. We did not dismiss it as a simple mistake nor condemn it as an act of stupidity. We figured out how to modify the attack play so fratricide would be near impossible.

Joe Moore recalled, "We learned to put terrain between ourselves on the attack and Alpha's overwatch. That way, even if they could see us, it was easier for them to orient toward the enemy."

We were out to win, and the AARs following simulated battles were crucial feedback mechanisms. In them, we would discuss what worked and what did not work in the just-finished battle. While such a process seems simple, the fact that we held AARs after every operation to discuss everything that happened made it clear that our actions mattered.

This was a marked contrast with the battalion to which my platoon had been cross-attached. In all of that task force's preparations, I had attended only one battalion-level AAR. I cannot remember anything specific about it, except that everything just seemed to be glossed over. The AARs with Dibella were memorable, in-depth, and incisive. The discussions resulted in actions and adjustments that made us better.

EVERYONE MATTERS

Dibella had a particular talent for making every element of our task force feel important. This was especially powerful in spreading the obsession to our cross-attached units. One former officer from our operations team recounted a notable example:

"When you think about the overall task force, the smoke platoon leader was not one of the guys who would come to mind in terms of importance. Rather, he was one of the guys who would be the last person you'd think of. That guy wasn't a tank company commander or an infantry company commander or the artillery battery commander; he was just the little ol' smoke platoon leader. But the way he was welcomed into everything and the detail that was put into his role was an indication of the attention to detail. He ended up playing an important role in the fights that we had. The guy understood what he was supposed to do and was fully committed to and vested in the team because of the way he was treated, brought in, and included in the process. The inclusiveness was really outstanding."

Even though we were in a peacetime Army, because of the empowerment, we felt as if our actions and our decisions had tremendous consequences. The simple measurement—did we win the battle or not?—gave immediate and effective feedback. It was a simple, powerful formula:

- Give people ownership in their results.
- Make the measurement of success simple and visible.
- Encourage everyone to learn from each other.
- Expect open and honest communication.
- Watch great things happen.

Even for the reluctant early skeptics, the high level of visibility and accountability drove the message home. Through the progression of many training exercises leading up to NTC, the level of ownership skyrocketed. The actions of your unit, your tank—even your own actions—might be discussed openly in the AAR. You mattered, and as the importance of winning every battle became a part of your DNA, you would do everything you could to make those victories happen. You had acquired the obsession.

14

AFFECTING LIVES
AND CAREERS IN 4-68

Fred Dibella often stated that combat effectiveness and combat readiness were the primary missions for a combat arms officer. He described the NTC as the finest military training facility in the history of the planet. But that was only partly how he felt about it. For him, it was not a place where 4-68 should go and learn how to be more combat effective; it was a place where 4-68 ought to go and *demonstrate* their combat effectiveness. NTC was a testing ground. The United States and Soviet Union were embroiled in the Cold War, and the fundamental mission for the US Army was to be prepared if hostilities erupted. For Dibella, the NTC rotation was our war. It was the place where we would prove—to ourselves and others—that we could fight and win World War III.

When Major General Bartlett told his new battalion commander to "Beat the OPFOR" and "Win at NTC," he was referring to what was, at the time, considered the extraordinarily remote possibility of gaining a positive winning percentage—winning five of the nine battles.

Dibella decided to double-down on the directive. As he saw it, "If our mission is to win at NTC, then *we will win at NTC*. Every battle—nine and oh."

The rationale he used drove home the message in a most personal and compelling way for the soldiers of Task Force 4-68. He presented it in clear and telling terms:

"In combat, do you plan on winning a 'majority' of your battles? Do you plan on accomplishing 'most' of your missions? Well, hell no. And why? Because when you lose in combat, you die! Your unit disappears. When you fail to accomplish your mission, the national security is at risk. Failure—losing even one battle—is just not an option."

The company commanders further galvanized the soldiers around this winning concept. Dave Carruthers, in front of Alpha Company, described it like this:

"If we ever go to war together, I refuse to consider the possibility of drafting letters to the family members of anyone in this company describing the circumstances of their death. We are Alpha Company. We are the killers, not the killed. NTC is our war. We are out to win. We will survive and kill the OPFOR."

The Silver Lions' logic was as simple as the well-known quote from General George S. Patton Jr. that was memorialized in the opening scene of the Academy Award–winning movie bearing his name: "No dumb bastard ever won a war by going out and dying for his country. He won it by making some other poor dumb bastard die for his country."

The trust and credibility Dibella built served to underline the very real threat we faced in the Cold War. Even though it was only a simulation, we felt the importance of winning at NTC as deeply as any peacetime Army unit could. No one in my platoon wanted to go to war with the battalion to which we were cross-attached for our first rotation. Our parent division had a very real mission in Europe in the event hostilities broke out. Being part of a task force that won only two of nine NTC battles would leave little confidence that we would survive even our first week in actual conflict, let alone accomplish our mission to defeat the Soviets. This internalization of the importance of winning at NTC brought out a level of energy in the soldiers that was magical.

The feeling was similar to the fiery determination the entire US population felt immediately after the attack on Pearl Harbor. Weeks before the attack, polls showed that 70 percent of the population wanted America to stay out of the war. Following December 7, 1941, every corner of this great country was awakened. People did extraordinary things because winning that war was not just all-important; it was the only thing that was important.

Housewives staffed factories. Volunteers flooded recruiting centers. Industries totally transformed to produce the machines of war. Everything became secondary to winning. The creative and industrial might of the nation accomplished in months or years what would have otherwise taken decades because of the impassioned energy directed toward the common goal. This is the type of energy and dedication Dibella harnessed within Task Force 4-68.

OPFOR'S LAST STAND

Our finest example of this esprit de corps was the final battle at NTC. Humiliated by 4-68's success against them, the OPFOR's pride and reputation were at stake. As 4-68 approached a winning record, the OPFOR commanders became doubly determined to embarrass the upstart battalion from Fort Carson. After eight successive victories, they tripled those efforts. In their view, 4-68 had been uncommonly lucky in its battles. They vowed this last battle would be different.

The two days between the eighth and ninth (final) battle gave the OPFOR the chance for special preparations. The simulated Soviet regiment would be on the attack, their favored type of operation. The engagement would take place on ground where they had seen great success against other opponents, plowing through battalion after battalion.

They knew the terrain and the routes into the objective that provided cover from defensive fire. They canceled leaves so that every OPFOR soldier would join the assault. For forty-eight straight hours, their maintenance groups worked around the clock. Every vehicle in their arsenal was repaired and ready for the offensive. They rolled more vehicles out of the assembly area for that battle than they ever had before. TF 4-68 would face the full strength of the OPFOR regiment.

We heard rumors through the Observer–Controllers of how the OPFOR was preparing for this final assault. The idea that the hitherto invincible OPFOR would pull out every stop in an attempt to defeat us was inspiring. We had won eight battles in a row, and there was no way our determined group of men would allow that last battle to slip from our fingers. Our preparations for the defense were the most intense ever.

At Piñon Canyon and earlier in the NTC rotation, we had experienced some difficulty convincing the engineers to precisely construct the type of two-tiered tank-fighting positions we wanted for the defense. The bulldozer operators tasked with creating these positions were cautious about digging too deep in the rough and rocky soil of the NTC and compromising their equipment. For this final defense, the bulldozer operators were even more exacting than the tank crews. They demanded that every position be tried and certified before considering it complete. In one day they dug twenty-eight perfect two-tiered fighting positions for Alpha Company, a feat the manuals would say takes several days.

Similar levels of effort were delivered throughout the task force. We put out obstacles and minefields to channel the OPFOR assault into our fields of fire. These were not simple fields of concertina wire; the obstacles our infantry companies and engineers constructed for that final battle were in harmony with Mother Earth. Only by knocking the planet off its axis would the OPFOR be able to plow through them. Preplanned artillery points were selected with great precision. Air defense and air support were rehearsed and rehearsed to a "gnat's ass."

Every one of our operating systems was working at its peak level in preparations for this final battle.

For Alpha Company, early in the morning we pulled back from our decoy positions into the well-dug tank foxholes that hid all but the commander's cupola. These expertly bulldozed defilade positions had two levels, one from which only the tank commander's torso could be seen from a distance and a second into which the tank could pull up, fully rotate its turret, and fire. The more forward decoy positions had only rudimentary preparations.

The OPFOR attack came at dawn. They had laid out a massive smoke screen to obscure our view of their march. It would have completely blocked our line of sight from the decoy positions. As the playbook directed, however, we were hundreds or thousands of meters from those locations, and our view was barely obscured. Nonetheless, the approaching OPFOR columns appeared daunting.

They came with three probing attacks with the rest of the regiment eager to reinforce and break through behind the most successful probe. Knowing that Soviet attack doctrine relied on speed and mass at the point of attack, we did not "wait until we saw the whites of their eyes"; we started firing as soon as the first vehicles came in range. Alpha Company engaged two of the probing armored columns; the third probe was headed toward the guns of our sister tank company.

It all happened very quickly. The accurate gunners of Alpha Company were a deadly force to meet on the open desert. We decimated the probing column to our left. The enemy probe to our right was taking fire, but the OPFOR knew this terrain and they had found cover in a *wadi*—a dry riverbed—that ran through the center of the task force's defensive position. We suspected they would try to run the entire regiment up this route.

Without hesitation, Captain Carruthers ordered my platoon to leave our dugout foxholes and cover the area where that wadi wound through the task-force defenses. The remaining Alpha Company assets would continue firing on the enemy forces that were rolling toward the riverbed's entrance.

As my platoon repositioned, Bravo Company had just finished taking out the probe to their front. The scouts radioed that the bulk of the regiment was on the move. Dibella and the company commanders concluded that the main enemy column would be coming up the central wadi. Bravo had clear lines of sight from their defensive position. My platoon reached a spot with good views into the wadi as well.

Those OPFOR vehicles that escaped the hail of fire from Alpha on their mad dash to the riverbed were massing for a determined run up the wadi. Undoubtedly they expected to break through by charging under its cover and then attacking our position from the rear. My platoon had seen a similar attack work with devastating effect in that first rotation. Unfortunately for the OPFOR, this time we had clear fields of fire.

The mass of simulated Soviet equipment became caught in a lethal crossfire between my platoon and the entire might of Bravo Company. These efforts would shortly be reinforced by elements of Delta Force and Charlie Mech.

Within half an hour, the battle was over. MILES lights were lit up throughout the OPFOR regiment, and 4-68 casualties were negligible. Despite all of the OPFOR preparations, we had the greatest margin of victory in this final battle. Thoughts that our success was due to a lucky streak were summarily put to rest.

We had done the impossible. The word quickly spread throughout the Army that an M60A3 task force from Fort Carson had gone 9–0 at the National Training Center. Later in the morning, I saw Dibella in his jeep. He was encouraging all the soldiers to savor the moment: "Every once in a while in life you get a chance to be a part of a great team. It may be a high school football team that wins a city championship or a summer little league program that gets first in the state. You remember them. This is one of those moments. You'll remember it for the rest of your life."

TRANSFORMATION

The difference between the 4-68 Armor that went to the National Training Center in April of 1986 and the one that listened to the auditorium presentation was profound. After months of training and drills, experimentation, refinement, and team building, the battalion had transformed into an unbeatable fighting machine. But there was no single event or inspirational moment that signaled the transition; it was a slow progression, day after day, slogging through the grind—constant and relentless training with emphases on finding ways to win and executing with precision.

All of this was worth it. Together we had achieved something extraordinary. This experience had a deep impact on many lives and subsequent careers. We had been through a transformative event, during which the least effective battalion in an Army division became the most lethal fighting task force in the US Army.

Dibella's hair always seemed to be in place, and his uniform somehow always seemed clean, but this was due to his intense attention to detail. We knew that in his heart he was also a soldier's soldier who could spit fire, get down in the mud, and wrestle with the best. The trust he built by acts of personal courage, such as the gunnery exercise only a few days after joining the battalion, gained him credibility in the eyes of even the most hardened soldiers. When he presented the goal of a 9–0 victory over OPFOR, it seemed impossible. But his words and actions constantly reinforced the idea that combat proficiency was the absolutely overriding priority. As we began to experience success, winning battles in training exercises at Fort Carson and Piñon Canyon, belief began to spread. With victory after victory, that belief grew into an obsession, and when we started beating the OPFOR at NTC, it became unstoppable.

Empowering an obsession that permeates an organization of more than 600 men is a monumental task if you had years to do it. Dibella did it in less than twelve months. The soldiers saw in Dibella someone they could respect, someone who would lead by example, and someone who they would follow. He offered a compelling vision of hope: Beat the OPFOR, and it will be something you can tell your grandchildren about. He offered stability from the high personnel turnover of the peacetime Army through his efforts to maintain consistency in the task force's organization and roles. He built trust through these actions of personal courage. Finally, he put the soldiers' welfare and sense of worth at the top of his priority list, creating an open and honest atmosphere of safety in communications that was uncommon in many military organizations.

You knew that he cared about each soldier and that he cared about you. These troops revered their commander much the way the Confederate soldiers revered General Thomas Jonathan "Stonewall" Jackson. Always out front, Jackson was mistakenly and mortally wounded by his own troops in the battle of Chancellorsville. Many historians speculate that if Jackson had been alive during the Battle of Gettysburg, that battle, and perhaps even the entire war, would have been a Confederate victory. The soldiers of 4-68 would follow Dibella into battle any day, any time, and against any foe.

15

ETHICS, INTENSITY, AND RESPECT AT STRYKER

John Brown's constantly communicated message of 20-percent growth epitomized the concept of focus. But even though such a clear definition of the organizational purpose unified the company, there was much more required to actualize the truly exceptional results Stryker delivered. Only when that goal became essential to a large percentage of the leaders and employees within the organization did the passion to achieve it become sustainable and virtually unstoppable. When the need to hit 20 percent became something vital—something we required of ourselves, something that defined personal and professional success—then it became something we would go to extraordinary lengths to achieve. It became a matter of deep personal and organizational commitment. Leaders and employees at all levels focused on whatever would lead to further growth. It became a shared obsession. By the end of John Brown's tenure, 20-percent growth was integral to the fabric of the organization and to the work ethic of thousands of Stryker employees.

As I mentioned earlier, Brown became CEO of Stryker following tragic circumstances when the company's founder and then-chairman, Dr. Homer Stryker, lost his only son, Lee, in an aviation accident. Lee had been president and CEO of the company and was actively involved in expanding into international markets and developing a direct sales team in the United States. It was a small firm, with about 300 employees, sales of $17 million, and an inventor/founder's mark clearly evident throughout the organization. The Stryker of 1977 was quite different from the lean, highly focused enterprise it would become.

I joined the company partway through that evolution. By 1989, Stryker had grown earnings 20 percent or more for twelve years, and company revenues were ten times what they were when Brown started. It was always engaging to hear the stories of his early days and the company's transformation into a growth machine. After having been a part of Task Force 4-68, the fundamental elements of that process sounded quite familiar.

Although it took place over decades, as opposed to one year, the foundations for empowering the organization with a pervasive and monomaniacal obsession to achieve such an extreme goal were quite similar to those of the Silver Lions. These bedrocks would serve to generate an extreme passion, affecting thousands of people for many years. Over three decades, Brown demonstrated an extraordinary commitment and earned a level of respect within the company that inspired confidence and belief. His personal dedication and work ethic were the stuff of legend, and they made an impact throughout the company. His determination attracted like-minded people—those who were eager to work hard, who wanted to see the fruits of their labors, and who had a burning ambition to be successful.

It was also remarkable that this obsession spread for decades even though the corporation had lacked a formal onboarding process outside of initial sales training. When I joined in 1989, there was no compelling multimedia presentation or cultlike indoctrination such as those used by many large companies to instruct new employees about their culture. You picked up the essence of what mattered because you were immediately immersed in it. The obsession to reach 20-percent growth spread like a virus from infected person to infected person. Once infected, you were forever altered. It became part of your DNA, and you became a carrier that would infect many more.

Leaders throughout the local community, in the churches and schools, noted how they could tell a Stryker person from others. At his last community presentation, Brown expressed this with his unique way of cutting to the essence: "If I was to explain our success with one statement, it would simply be that Stryker people are different!"

DEMONSTRATING A TIRELESS WORK ETHIC

Brown grew up as the oldest of five children in the farmlands of Tennessee, where early mornings, long days, and tough physical labor were the norm. Although his personal fortune grew, he maintained a very modest lifestyle. He lived in the same Portage, Michigan, home he had first moved into in 1977. He drove simple cars, such as the Ford Taurus, and he would fly coach in accordance with company policy until his airline miles accrued enough to gain free upgrades through the frequent-flyer programs. Many times he was awarded the top or near-top status in surveys regarding the efficiency of CEO pay—the best shareholder returns for the money paid in CEO compensation. Although he was always well dressed and groomed, he simply showed no hubris. When Brown retired, the board of directors collected personal funds to give him a luxury car; otherwise, it is likely he never would have owned one.

For many, the simple, hardworking approach to life and career that John Brown personified was a significant factor in their decisions to join the organization. It formed a cornerstone of the type of commitment that catalyzed spreading of the company's obsession. In many discussions with those who personally interviewed with Brown while being recruited into the company, this theme repeated. They expressed a sense of connection with him and a deep sincerity in the interview conversation. These conversations often made a lasting impact. One highly respected engineering leader who retired after a forty-year career noted three turning points of his career. His most memorable was the immediate impact and sense of responsibility he felt during his interview with John Brown.

Another highly respected divisional vice president said of his interview, "We just had a conversation. He asked about my upbringing. He grew up on a farm; I grew up on a farm. He understood the nature of work for a farmer, that effort and sacrifice were part of the everyday experience, that working hard is just what you did. I respected that."

My own experience was similar. We talked about my family background, and I explained some of my father's career history. Dave Morton went to college on the GI Bill; graduated as an electrical engineer from a Big Ten school; and joined what, at the time, seemed like a bastion of American industrial strength—the steel industry. Over forty years he poured great effort into his work. He modeled a dedicated work ethic, constantly answering calls at all hours of the evening and never complaining about late nights and weekends. Unfortunately, in the industry he chose all that effort could not stem the company's decline. I was looking for a place where such efforts might make a difference and lead to success. During my Saturday morning interview, I couldn't help but give Brown instant respect as a leader with an appetite for hard work that already demonstrated a clear tie between that work and success.

Similar to Fred Dibella's demonstrations of personal courage, John Brown's demonstrations of a tireless work ethic were a bonding force within the organization. It helped to inspire like-minded people to join and to create a hardworking environment within the organization. Brown often used the president's message in the company's annual report to echo this sentiment.

In 1983's report, he wrote, "At Stryker, we are fortunate to have a staff distinguished by dedication and reliability. We depend on our people."

In 1992's, he wrote, "I want to thank Stryker's employees at all levels for the talent and hard work that have given us another excellent year."

In 1997's: "We appreciate the hard work and dedication of our employees, management, and board of directors."

And in 2001: "I want to thank our shareholders for their confidence in the company and our employees for their hard work."

The phrase *hard work* resonates throughout the company's history and throughout Brown's letters.

John Brown deeply believed that setting an example of a dedicated work ethic would have far-reaching effects.

"I believe in setting a good example," he said. "I tried very hard, and worked very hard, but I enjoyed it. I think that has a great influence on your colleagues and subordinates. They know that you're really sincere about the company's success, that you'll do anything that you can do and have to do to make it successful. And it draws a special kind of person to the organization."

Such an example must somehow tap into our primate psychology and alleviate doubts to know that the leader will not ask anyone to endure a hardship they would not endure themselves. John Brown's work ethic and visible demonstrations of commitment to the 20-percent growth objective were essential elements in spreading an ethos that the goal was worth extreme effort, and they became doubly influential when paired with an intensity to win.

A WINNER'S INTENSITY

A dogged determination to win was pervasive within Stryker's employee base. In the early 2000s, the company commissioned an outside consulting group to study all the divisions and provide a framework to help define the Stryker brand and what made the company special. In the view of most insiders, the consultants did excellent work describing Stryker's pillars of success. One of these key pillars was "a winner's intensity."

In this same time period, I attended a professional-development session where one of Gallup's most respected analysts described many things about Stryker and the people within the company. One of his most cogent statements was that of all the groups, teams, and companies for which they had data, "Stryker was simply the most fiercely competitive organization on the planet." He went on to explain the many ways in which the concept of winning was so deeply interwoven into the culture of the company. It was a fundamental part of the profiles and personality makeup of its leaders. Stryker's prevalence of competitive themes in the profiles of its leaders was so far outside the mean that it seemed almost unreal, even statistically impossible.

Stryker's fierce decentralization added to the winner's intensity by bringing visibility to comparative results. Divisional performance was exposed and ranked. The measurements were unequivocal, objective, and apolitical. This ultratransparency existed before the term *transparency* came in vogue, and Brown explained this part of the company's purpose in the 1985 annual report:

"It is our belief that this new structure will bring clear progress toward corporate and divisional objectives, based on shared managerial responsibilities both up and down the line."

A huge part of ensuring that clarity was measuring progress and providing visibility to it. Every meaningful measurement of success was *racked and stacked* at Stryker. As we discussed earlier, the extreme was in sales performance. Every month all the reps were ranked in their divisions for the month and year-to-date in measures of total order dollars, percentage growth, and percent to quota. Sales regions were racked and stacked for the monthly financial reviews. Divisional sales teams were racked and stacked by growth in John Brown's monthly management letter. This letter also ranked every sales regional manager by his or her year-to-date growth. Manufacturing plants were racked and stacked by their on-time order-fulfillment percentages. Your team's results were visible every single month.

Every division coveted the top position. Although outsiders often criticized such competition as too internally focused, Brown later explained it this way: "The whole idea of building the internal competition was to sharpen and hone our skills so we could take on the outside competition. That was the whole concept of setting up the hierarchy, rewarding those over 20 percent, scolding those under 20. The idea was to make us sharper and sharper and sharper so that we could beat the external competition."

The financial growth each division generated provided a measurement of our efforts and a means of comparison to sister divisions. This internal competition was fierce and inspiring.

There is perhaps no better example of this winner's intensity than the saga of the company's entry into the general patient care or medical–surgical bed market. This saga exemplifies the fanatical nature of Stryker's will to win and John Brown's capacity to persevere. The story is not one of instant success, but it does illustrate Stryker's obsession to achieve 20-percent earnings growth against the most daunting odds.

CHALLENGING GIANTS

To set the historical context, the battle began in the early 1980s. Hill-Rom, the venerable healthcare division of Fortune 500 company Hillenbrand Industries, had pushed its final competitor out of the US hospital bed market and controlled a virtual monopoly. Their only challenge came from the small Kalamazoo upstart, Stryker, which began to develop some niche products for high-demand areas of the hospital underserved by Hill-Rom's general-care beds.

The most threatening of these niche products was a specialty bed Stryker had custom designed for Intensive Care Units (ICU) and launched in the early 1980s. Stryker's 938 bed included breakthrough features such as in-bed scales and the ability to x-ray the patient without removing them from the bed—allowing in-bed fluoroscopy for the first time ever.

THE GIANT AWAKENS

Hill-Rom took notice and embarked on a mission to crush Stryker's beachhead in ICU. The much larger (at the time) company was absolutely determined to maintain its monopoly position. They adopted a two-pronged approach. First, they began developing their own specialty beds, including those for the ICU, that would leapfrog Stryker's offerings. Second, they embarked on an all-out offensive to attack Stryker's core stretcher market and rob the upstart of its primary source of cash and earnings.

In late 1985, Hill-Rom launched the GPS, a mobile hospital stretcher that was height-adjustable through the use of hydraulics; and this stretcher had several feature advantages over Stryker's current products. Touting its lower height when collapsed, tuck-away side rails that reduced the gap between surfaces for patient transfers, and an all-around bumper system, Hill-Rom's sales team could bundle the GPS with their beds in large deals. It was Hill-Rom's first entry into Stryker's core market, where the larger company planned to commoditize the hospital stretcher segment and wreck Stryker's profit base for developing specialty beds. The challenge issued at Hill-Rom's annual sales meeting when they launched the GPS was to put Stryker out of business.

Given a few feature advantages and their industry-leading sales team with deep relationships in hospital administrations, Hill-Rom put Stryker's Medical Division stretcher sales under pressure. Compounding the situation, the larger competitor's new customized ICU bed technologically leapfrogged Stryker's 938, and Stryker's launch of a radically different electromechanical ICU bed was plagued by technical problems. As this battle unfolded in the mid- to late 1980s, Hill-Rom captured a chunk of the stretcher market and became the leader in ICU. Stryker's Medical Division, a former bastion of growth and profitability, was struggling; Hill-Rom posed a genuine threat to the 20-percent growth streak.

STRYKER COUNTERATTACKS

John Brown took action. Over twenty years later, he would recall, "During that same period, Hill-Rom, at the time, really thought they could put us out of business."

Stryker's standing Medical Division president retired, and Brown hired Harry Carmitchel, who had turned around wheelchair maker Everest & Jennings's business in the early 1980s. Carmitchel's challenge was to retake lost market share and go on the offensive against Hill-Rom. He set out to build a new divisional leadership team. He recruited sales, marketing, and operations leaders—many from his former E&J team. They were able to slow the progress of Hill-Rom's assault in stretchers. The Medical Division then responded with the Renaissance Series: A new ICU bed and an innovative new line of emergency- and recovery-room stretchers in 1990.

With the sales and marketing team under solid leadership, the new ICU bed technically sound, and orders for the new stretcher line recapturing lost market share, the Medical Division's revenues began to grow again. But the all-important earnings were still under pressure.

As sales continued to improve, I had the opportunity to manage three interdisciplinary teams in a comprehensive, multiyear design, manufacturing, and reengineering program that dramatically improved the division's cost position. These teams designed-in cost effectiveness, drove product quality improvements, and introduced manufacturing process innovations, all of which allowed the division to set a new bar for its historically strong gross margins.

By late 1991, Medical was seen as a fantastic turnaround story. The division stood atop many of Stryker's internal rankings, orders were flowing in, costs were down, margins were up, and manufacturing was humming. We had proven that Hill-Rom could be beaten and that the stolid old metal benders of the Medical Division could keep pace with the growth that our Surgical counterparts were generating in surgical instruments and the fast-growing endoscopy market.

Carmitchel's senior team was still concerned about Hill-Rom's ambitions in the stretcher market and knew they needed to find new growth opportunities if Medical was to keep up. Deciding to go on the offensive, Carmitchel made a momentous decision to take the battle to Hill-Rom.

A FULL-FRONTAL ASSAULT

As Hill-Rom had done with stretchers in the mid-1980s, Stryker's Medical Division would develop and launch a product attacking Hill-Rom's core medical–surgical bed market. To provide focus and minimize distraction for those delivering 20-percent earnings growth in existing product lines, Medical formed a sizable off-site development team, with the mission to develop and launch an innovative medical–surgical bed and attack Hill-Rom.

Stryker's board of directors and John Brown were told that the attack was going into an exposed flank of the enemy, who would be unable to respond. The official plan was to masterfully develop a product so advanced and innovative that it would be able to combine the hospital bed market with what, at the time, was a high-tech specialty rental-bed market comprised of specialized beds with advanced surfaces that had skin-to-surface-pressure–reducing technologies. Stryker's new combination would include many of the benefits of the expensive rental beds and would be the best medical–surgical bed ever made. The value proposition to hospital customers would be infinitely compelling. By replacing their general-care beds with this advanced product, they could revitalize their floors and save millions in rental fees. Hill-Rom would be trapped, because they had built an immense infrastructure to support the rental-bed market.

It all sounded good, but the realities of executing such an ambitious plan would far overreach the technical capability of Stryker or any other company at the time. It would be nearly a decade before the technology existed to build such a device. The plan was tantamount to attempting development of the iPod in 1985, long before miniature hard drives, flash memory, high-speed PC connectivity, or energy-efficient microprocessors existed in any meaningful form. A dreadful feeling hit the pit of my stomach after the off-site team asked me to come over and complete a cost estimate of their new bed. Seeing the amount of work they had on their plate, it was clear that just completing the bed would consume that team's resources and that the visionary product was years away.

Using an American Civil War analogy, the plan was akin to Pickett's Charge—a frontal assault by many of the army's most valuable assets across an open field into the heart of a well-prepared and entrenched enemy. Hill-Rom's mid-1980s thrust into stretchers was similar in nature. However, their attack into the smaller stretcher market was not the main event. It was a frontal assault, but along a narrow axis; and they did make flanking maneuvers on the product side with new features and on the sales side by capitalizing on their administrative relationships. Moreover, Hill-Rom was not gambling with the core of their army. For Stryker, as for Lee's army at Gettysburg, launching the medical–surgical bed would be the main event.

Humanity's long history of warfare demonstrates that full-frontal assaults of this nature seldom succeed. The defender has every advantage. The demise of the Confederacy's infamous attack during the third day at Gettysburg turned the tide of the war. Before the ill-fated charge, the Confederate army knew only victory. Following the charge, they would know only defeat.

In warfare, such actions result in a tragic loss of lives. The carnage of countless ill-fated assaults across no-man's-land between the trenches of WWI provides perhaps the most gruesome examples. In business, these actions result in lost money, ruined careers, and painful personal hardship for the attackers.

After I completed the estimate, which projected that the product would come in way over its target cost, I lost the ear of the Patient Care leadership. Not wanting to face reality, they discounted the high estimate, rationalizing that it did not accurately portray the advantages of the bed's volume production processes, which were new to Stryker.

As was Robert E. Lee on the dawn of Gettysburg's third day, they were convinced their plan would succeed despite ominous indications to the contrary. I hesitated to openly express further concerns about the plan, because it was clear I had no audience. Telling Pickett's troops that they were doomed would only dampen their enthusiasm—which was perhaps the only asset they had that morning. I hoped that I was wrong and that somehow, in the fog of the upcoming battle, the sales team might charge fast enough and find hidden vulnerabilities in Hill-Rom's fortifications.

The bed division's leadership believed the force of their frontal assault would carry the day. The ingenious product that would combine two markets could wait; they were confident that the talented Patient Care sales team would win with the better, more innovative bed. As customers began previewing the product, enthusiasm heightened. The unique networking technology, lower height, modern appearance, optional in-bed scales, bed-exit warning systems, and other technological advances gained positive customer reviews. Banking their success on dozens of such small advantages defined this as a direct frontal assault.

To win, however, Stryker had to convince executives in a hospital's C-suite that the Stryker bed was worth trying. With no compelling differentiated technology that resonated with hospital leadership, the two dozen small feature improvements were unconvincing. Even though the floor nurses generally preferred our bed, the administration was closely tied to Hill-Rom. Buying new beds was a fifteen- to twenty-year commitment, and most saw no credible reason to take a risk on Stryker. Hill-Rom was also well prepared for the assault. When the valiant Stryker bed sales team charged into no-man's-land, they were met with the full force and ferocity of Hill-Rom's marketing and sales might. The company had not become a near monopoly because they easily gave up ground in their homeland.

Hill-Rom had world-class information systems, with a complete view of the type and age of beds for every hospital in the country. Every time their sales and marketing leadership discovered that Stryker was in an account, they moved swiftly to block. They had the ear of hospital administration and would sow seeds of doubt about Stryker's quality, offer lower prices, bundle other products into the deal, or renegotiate with significant trade-in allowances.

Stryker's Patient Care Division found itself stuck with a product whose cost came in 70 percent over target, with high-cost features for which hospital administrators were unwilling to pay a premium. The threat of "Hillarycare" loomed, which would have narrowed hospital operating margins across the country, and hospitals were becoming more cost conscious. Stryker's Patient Care salespeople became so desperate for orders that they sold the beds for 30 percent less than Hill-Rom was getting prior to our market entry. To make matters even worse, Stryker's bed had to undergo a massive recall shortly after the first units were shipped. In short, a year after the sales launch, like Pickett's valiant Georgians, the battlefield was littered with exhausted Stryker salespeople, tired-out service technicians performing recalls, and a demoralized home office. The Medical Division's profits were suffering, and the Patient Handling (stretcher) business was strained to the breaking point by making up for the shortfalls in Patient Care.

REGROUPING AND REINFORCING

In Pickett's ill-fated charge, the Confederates had no choice but to sound the retreat, salvage what they could of the Army of Northern Virginia, and march back to the South. At Stryker, however, that was not our way.

The winner's intensity kicked into overdrive. This was a growth company, 20 percent was the law, and the bed was planned to be a significant contributor to that growth. Stryker kept the assault going, and John Brown had put a picture of the new medical–surgical bed on the cover of the 1993 annual report, signifying the company's commitment to the market. Like the determined World War I generals who believed another assault by fresh troops would carry the day, Stryker kept attacking—convinced that if we worked hard enough and long enough, success would come.

The Medical Division received a great deal of "help" from Corporate. The first moves were to replace many of the Patient Care leadership who bailed as their strategy's demise became evident. I was moved from Patient Handling to Patient Care to lead the R&D and manufacturing–engineering effort. My team's primary mission was to reengineer the bed and its manufacturing for lower costs and improved quality. A new sales leader was brought in who knew the market and could recruit top-caliber sales talent. Carmitchel, the Medical Division president, assumed the vacated leadership position for Patient Care. We all worked incredibly long hours and poured extraordinary passion into the business. We made great progress with a host of initiatives, but the fundamental strategy in the medical–surgical market remained a frontal assault.

Desperate to salvage the division's profitability, the teams under me cut the bed's cost dramatically and vertically integrated its manufacturing, but this was not enough. It remained a more feature-laden bed selling at a lower price than the market leader's, and Hill-Rom was more aggressive than ever in every competitive account. They made quick design changes to their main beds, matching many of Stryker's new features, covering any slightly exposed flank. Adding to our frustration, Hill-Rom was able to convince many customers that the changes they made to catch up with Stryker's bed were Hill-Rom's innovations and not Stryker's. The new sales VP hired people better suited for the ferocity of competing with Hill-Rom, but this was not enough. The individual Stryker reps were fighting fanatically, like Leonidas's famous 300 Spartans at Thermopylae. And like the doomed Spartans, the sheer numbers and resources of Hill-Rom's army seemed too much to overcome.

But this was Stryker; this was a company that grew by 20 percent every quarter, every year. It was a company with a winner's intensity, and we continued the fight. John Brown and a team from Corporate met every week with the Patient Care leadership to monitor progress. These were dubbed the *bed-rock* meetings. With an obvious dual meaning—maybe we were about to "rock" the bed market, or maybe we were the clumsy characters from the Flintstones cartoon, not really certain what we were doing. Brown soon recognized that a product to combine the rental and bed markets was simply a pipe dream. This left Patient Care in a desperate situation. Cornered in what seemed an unwinnable scenario, I saw the absolutely iron will of John Brown most forcibly expressed. He simply would not give up. Through it all, he maintained faith that we would find a path to success, no matter what. He maintained the belief that talented troops committed to the cause would gain a rightful share of the market.

In 1983's annual report, Brown had written, "Our strategy is really quite simple. It is to pick a niche market and apply our considerable talent, knowledge, and experience to [inventing, making, and selling the product]."

By the early 1990s, growth had made the requirement to enter main-stream markets inevitable; the niches were simply not large enough. With the medical–surgical assault, Stryker found a division embroiled in a fight for its life in such a mainstream market. Other divisions were successful in attacking mainstream markets, as their growth require-ments naturally led them into the fray. However, none of those was against a single, monolithic competitor in a capital-goods-only market. Stryker's other markets were more fragmented. As divisions attacked these mainstream markets, their sales and marketing teams would fig-ure out how to win against competitor A, B, or C. The grand strategy at the divisional level was secondary to dogged execution by the individual sales rep and through product features.

In the difficult med-surg bed market, John Brown remained con-vinced that "no market is going to give 100 percent of the business to the same company. If we just focus on keeping our head down, focusing on innovation and fighting account by account, market by market, we [will] gain a respectable share."

As the battle continued, we poured every effort into beating Hill-Rom, but it was not enough. Twelve months after I moved to Patient Care, it became clear that the fresh troops were not gaining ground against the behemoth Hill-Rom sales and marketing machine, although some things were improving. The revised bed's cost was much closer to its original target, and after a few bumps getting the software completed we could mass-produce them with high quality.

The deliberate design for manufacturability executed by these teams was extraordinary. US Amada, a world-class machine-tool company, cited Patient Care's manufacturing plant as a best-in-class example of one-piece flow and cellular manufacturing. Nonetheless, the turnover in the sales team and huge issues with bed pricing were simply daunting. Patient Care was still losing money with every bed shipped. It was time to call a temporary retreat and reorganize.

RESHAPING THE BATTLE

At this point, John Brown made decisions to ensure the assault against the Hill-Rom medical–surgical bed's market position would no longer be the main event for an entire division. Carmitchel moved on to opportunities beyond Stryker. In a highly countercultural move, Brown recombined the Patient Care and Patient Handling divisions. For this newly united Medical Division, the frontal attack in the medical–surgical market would still be a significant event, but it would no longer put the entire division on the line as it had for Patient Care. He brought in Brian Hutchison as Medical's president to get things in order. Hutchison had an accounting background, along with prior experience in Medical. He quickly made the difficult but necessary moves to stop us from hemorrhaging cash.

Hutchison conducted a major employee reduction in force, cleared out the leadership ranks at Patient Care, and proceeded to hire another new leadership team. As the only VP-level survivor, I once again joined a talented team that came together, formed very close bonds, and committed themselves to winning in the bed and stretcher markets. Brown kept the pressure on from Corporate. He had confidence in Hutchison, and the focus was now two-pronged: Make progress against Hill-Rom in medical–surgical beds, but also stem the financial bleeding and exploit growth opportunities in many of our other product lines. This new team bonded together in the face of daunting odds and committed to the challenging fight.

In a fortuitous move, Hutchison moved Scott Giambalvo, the marketing lead from my EMS start-up group, to manage marketing for the ill-fated bed. Giambalvo had helped draft a successful attack against another monopoly competitor in EMS. That monopoly player, Ferno-Washington, was not as large or as revered as Hill-Rom, but Ferno had fought its way to a dominating position in ambulance stretchers, fastening systems, chairs, and other apparatuses during the same period when Hill-Rom was establishing its dominance in the US hospital bed market. Ferno had also done it on a global basis, gaining market share of 80–90 percent in nearly all the developed world's prehospital markets.

Unlike the bed frontal assault, we had attacked a vulnerable flank in that monopoly's otherwise impressive market position. We had massed our efforts on this weakness, and the EMS product line was doing well. Knowing that success was unlikely if he promoted a better bed against the monolithic leader beloved by hospital administration, Giambalvo devoted himself to identifying a critical weakness in Hill-Rom's strength.

He studied the few talented sales reps who had figured out ways to succeed in the medical–surgical market. Reflecting on their success, he renamed and repositioned the bed. It became the Stryker Secure bed. A key patented technology we had was a bed-exit warning system that would actually indicate when a patient might be about to fall out of bed. Hill-Rom had unreliable bed-exit technology that raised an alarm only after the patient had already fallen. As patients became more and more acute in America's hospitals, the issue of falls was gaining heightened awareness. Progressive hospitals began to understand that falls were costing them and the healthcare system millions of dollars.

Hutchison's new marketing VP then focused on teaming with

leading hospitals in efforts to reduce patient falls, with Stryker's technology at the forefront. We developed compelling sales tools and marketing programs that were all about positioning Stryker as the safe, secure alternative, with proprietary technology that could help dramatically reduce patient falls and address other patient-safety issues that were problems with Hill-Rom's beds.

Finally, we were massing our efforts around a crucial and highly differentiated feature of the bed. Even reluctant hospital administrators began to see Stryker's offering as dramatically different. Similar to what we had done in EMS, we concentrated our efforts on that difference. We were no longer attempting to be a better Hill-Rom with a bed that had incremental improvements in three dozen areas. Instead the sales focus shifted to going after hospitals that could understand and look for solutions to issues with patient safety. Of course, Hill-Rom countered, offering their bed-exit technology virtually for free or claiming that their beds were the most proven. The problem was that Hill-Rom's technology, particularly with regard to bed-exit warnings and side-rail systems, lacked crucial functions. We had found an exposed flank.

Sales reps who embraced the Secure concept and pushed the bed-exit system started to see success. They even sold beds for a small profit. However, the newly recombined division's sales leader, an aggressive, highly confident transplant from General Electric, did not connect with the plight of his troops. He assumed a negative view of many of the bedside veterans and sales managers. Many of the best reps left for greener pastures, and those who stayed became increasingly disengaged.

Turnover in sales was taking its toll. Hutchison replaced the sales VP and gave an internal transfer the mission to salvage the disheartened team. The Stryker Secure was the right move to make, but it was like showing up in the trenches of World War I with a modern battle tank and trying to get the same exhausted, demoralized soldiers to conduct a World War II–style blitzkrieg. Exploiting the Secure concept would require new leadership that was not bruised by frustrated memories of the frontal assault.

RETAKING THE INITIATIVE

Looking back in 2015, while discussing our fight against Hill-Rom, Brown recalled, "They were better at marketing and sales during that ten-year run" (1989–1999).

Hutchison's team had gotten the *invent it* and *make it* parts of the bed business in reasonable shape when Brown made another move in the late 1990s that would significantly turn the tide. Stryker was in the middle of acquiring implant maker Howmedica and engaged in the monumental task of integrating an organization nearly as large as itself. As part of the process, Medical moved into a group of divisions called the Medical–Surgical Group (not to be confused with the medical–surgical bed). This group included many of the legacy businesses of the company, including Medical, Instruments, and Endoscopy. Leading the group was Ron Elenbaas, the longtime and highly successful president of the former Stryker Surgical Group and likely heir apparent to John Brown. Brown knew Elenbaas was a sales guru, and the divisions under him had built several of the best sales teams in the company.

This was the first time I had the chance to work with Elenbaas, and it quickly became another highlight of my Stryker experience. He came in with a larger-than-life personal charisma and a winner's attitude—just what our weary team needed. We will cover this sales transformation in later chapters. Suffice it to say here that over the next decade, Stryker would become a major force in the medical–surgical bed business, eventually gaining over 50-percent market share. When combined with its market-leading stretcher product line and the highly innovative EMS business, Medical would post company-leading, gold-standard 20-percent growth for nearly a decade.

As Brown recalled, "Over time, we got better and better at sales, too.

With our innovation and a good sales and marketing effort, we started to catch market share."

In the final analysis, Stryker did the impossible: We won Pickett's Charge through sheer will and determination. The simple *invent it, make it, sell it* approach eventually prevailed. After years of hurling salespeople headlong into the enemy fortifications, incurring more than $20 million in losses in 1995 and cycling through multiple leadership teams, 99 percent of companies would have given up on the effort. Such a concession was not in Stryker's collective blood and not something John Brown would accept. Beaten back for year after year, Stryker just kept coming. Eventually the sales and marketing teams found weaknesses in Hill-Rom's position. Once we established a beachhead and poured the right troops into it, the Medical–Surgical group's offense focused on the basics and became unstoppable.

This story, while fraught with mistakes and missteps, illustrates the irresistible energy that empowering an obsession can bring to a team. I was part of four teams at Stryker Medical that were totally engaged and 100-percent committed to beating Hill-Rom and delivering on the 20-percent promise. Each of these teams banded together and gave every ounce of creativity and determination they had for the cause. The autonomy and authority given to us served to build a pronounced level of ownership and commitment. We were fighting a desperate battle, but it was *our* battle. In a sense, we went through hell together.

EARNED RESPECT, PERSEVERANCE, AND PERSONAL CONTACT

Although the assault on Hill-Rom's monopoly position in the medical–surgical bed market was not his idea, it was a testament to the respect for John Brown's leadership that four distinct teams acquired the obsession and plunged headlong into the battle in the relentless pursuit of 20-percent growth. Only a small number of salespeople and leaders stayed (or were able to stay) with Stryker to experience the entire saga of the assault on Hill-Rom from its inception to its final success. To a person, that group had developed a deep and genuine respect for John Brown.

Despite all the personnel changeover, leadership turmoil, and personal hardships we lived through, Brown always maintained his belief and focus on inventing great products for our customers, manufacturing them with high quality, and selling them through talented sales teams. Even with numerous analyst pleas to sell the Medical business, Brown's commitment to winning the battle and beating Hill-Rom was unwavering. The leadership changeovers and bed-rock meetings were not the types of interactions any executive hoped to have with Mr. Brown, but they did illustrate an iron will and an absolutely maniacal obsession to win.

This type of respect for John Brown echoed through the many divisional sales teams. In January of every year, Stryker divisions held their annual sales meetings. Every sales representative and sales manager attended. All around the world, the divisions coordinated meeting plans so that Brown could attend. At two events, salespeople would have the chance to interact with the CEO. The first of these was the awards ceremony and the reception immediately prior.

On numerous occasions, salespeople would recount their astonishment at their interactions with Brown. They told stories of how they had a discussion with Brown one year, and two or three years later they would have the chance to talk with him again. He would ask them something about the conversation they had at the prior meeting. In Brown's latter years, when Stryker had well over 1,000 sales reps throughout all its divisions, Brown maintained those connections. For the salespeople, tales of this remarkable ability earned great respect.

The second sales meeting event was only for the quota achievers, who were invited to attend the Chairman's Breakfast. This took place at 6:00 a.m. sharp on the morning following the official awards ceremony. There was such respect for Brown and his work ethic that no one would show up late, no matter how long they had been up celebrating the night before. After a delicious meal and a champagne toast, each rep would receive their annual bonus check directly from the chairman, but only after they spoke to the group. Some of the speeches were like Academy Award acceptances, but the ones Brown enjoyed the most were about beating the competition in important deals. The checks would go out in order of achievement, with the top achiever speaking last and getting the most attention. For large divisions, these breakfasts could last up to four hours. Brown stood, handed out the checks, and tirelessly announced the achievers' names, often including a personal anecdote about those he knew from prior breakfasts. Even the most cynical noted the clear display of Brown's work ethic. All of it served to further empower frontline sales personnel to work hard and return for the breakfast the following year.

These demonstrations of work ethic and an indomitable will to win from the company CEO were infectious. Just as Fred Dibella earned credibility and respect within Task Force 4-68, John Brown earned a deep trust over nearly three decades with thousands of Stryker employees. This trust amplified the sense of empowerment and ownership brought by rigorous decentralization. Even in the darkest days of Medical's fight against Hill-Rom, the leadership at Medical felt ownership for the fight. The bed-rock meetings did not decrease accountability; they made the teams *more* accountable. Brown was there to rally additional resources and bring swift decision-making to actions the team believed would drive success. Everything was set up to empower the 20-percent obsession.

16

STABILITY

AT STRYKER

Although the multiple changes in Medical Division's management during the battle with Hill-Rom may make it sound as though Stryker was a churn-and-burn enterprise, the company benefited from many underlying threads of consistency and stability that were crucial to empowering the 20-percent obsession. During the John Brown era, a simple and consistent philosophy and approach to issues served as a compass—clearly defining true north.

Even though John Brown had a reputation as a tough taskmaster and Stryker was occasionally criticized in the local community for having high personnel turnover in this era, the facts paint a different story. At his direct-report level, which included the division presidents and chief financial officer, Brown's team was actually a model of stability. Of the nine operating divisions that comprised the company when I joined, eight of their presidents were still in place ten years later; and as we discussed in the last chapter, the one who resigned had gotten his division into an impossible situation. During this period the company moved into the

Fortune 500 and became one of the most respected medical-device firms in the world. Often overlooked in analyses of Stryker's success, such stability in the leadership was highly correlated with the company's financial performance, as well as to that of each division.

The average age of an employee at the company was quite young. This could create the perception that experience was not valued. However, the simple mathematics of growth reveals the truth:

Stryker's environment took time to internalize, and the company generally promoted from within its own ranks. To fill the positions created from growth, most hiring was done either at the entry level or for candidates with five to ten years of experience—still fairly young. The company was doubling in size every 3.7 years. Given the positive hire-from-within dynamic for existing employees, even with headcount growing slower than earnings, this typically meant that more than half of the employees were new every five years. Stryker did hire some highly experienced people from outside, and folks did retire or move on— especially in sales; but for most on the factory floor, the company was a highly reliable source of employment. This stability paid great dividends.

MORE STABILITY—MORE EARNINGS

For many years Medical's counterpart in Kalamazoo, the Surgical Instruments Division, was the go-to business for making up the deficit created by the challenges in entering the hospital bed market. Instruments' long run in the 1990s is perhaps the best illustration of how close-knit and—unlike Medical—stable teams, empowered by the 20-percent obsession, delivered astounding results.

Instruments grew out of a subset of the product lines that were part of the Surgical business following the Medical–Surgical split in the mid-1980s. Surgical delivered its 20-percent earnings growth in the years immediately following the split by expanding its product offerings through a combination of internal development and key acquisitions. At the end of the 1980s, the business was participating in two fairly distinct markets, and it further split into the legacy-powered Surgical Instruments Division, headquartered in Kalamazoo, and the burgeoning new Endoscopy Division, which set roots in Silicon Valley. Si Johnson, a Kalamazoo native who had a long history of success in sales and marketing at Stryker, would lead Instruments.

Within a relatively short time, Johnson settled on his senior leaders, and this team coalesced into a 20-percent obsessed, high-performance organization. Over the next ten years, Stryker Instruments would grow to dominate many of the markets in which it competed. The division was perhaps the archetypical example of what John Brown would later describe as a transformational time for the company. He characterized the 1989–1999 period as the *long run*, "a period when Stryker went from being this quaint little company out of Kalamazoo, Michigan, that made a cast cutter, a turning frame, and a few other things to a very powerful medical-device company. And so the competition went from amusement to respect to fear. The 20-percent goal was twice to three times the rate of growth of the competition, so the only way to do it was to gobble up market share."

Instruments was at the tip of the spear, delivering exceptional results throughout this long run. The division was among the first to understand the criticality of talent and to develop powerful tools to help attract, manage, and retain highly talented people. Team stability was not often verbalized as an important tenet in its organizational strategy. However, for empowering the 20-percent obsession, talent was only one element of the equation. Experience, familiarity with each other, trust earned over time, and team dynamics—all things that come with stability—also made a huge impact.

During the decade of the long run, Instruments' leadership team was highly stable. The senior leader for each leg of the *invent it, make it, sell it* stool remained consistent throughout the run. R&D, manufacturing, and sales enjoyed a powerful level of interdependence and mutual respect, partially brought about by the leadership stability.

The Instruments team enjoyed high camaraderie, familiarity with each other's strengths and weaknesses, and a commitment to shared success. When asked to deliver earnings above their 20-percent plan, they bonded together and figured it out time and time again. Years later, members of that team fondly recounted the high level of trust and genuine concern for each other's success in that highly stable team.

Johnson was a strong advocate of the importance of talent, and I sensed he felt responsible to have not just a stable team but also have the best possible person in each position on his leadership team. Nonetheless, with the performance they were delivering year after year, he did not make any significant changes to his direct team. Later, in the post–John Brown era, the teams for divisions within Johnson's group saw considerable change and turnover; none experienced the stability that his team at Instruments had enjoyed in the 1990s. The divisional performance was not as consistent, either.

After figuring out how to sell medical–surgical beds, the Medical Division was a top performer from 1999 to 2009. For all of the success in that decade, Medical still struggled in the highly interdependent activity of delivering earnings—the cornerstone of 20 percent. All three legs of the *invent it, make it, sell it* stool need to be on solid ground and working together in lockstep to meet an earnings plan year after year. As the Medical leadership team underwent considerable change during that period, the bed-stretcher part of the business consistently struggled to deliver its earnings numbers. The EMS business within Medical, which enjoyed great stability in the *invent it* and *sell it* parts of its leadership team over this time, was able to overdeliver earnings for nearly a decade to make up the shortfalls.

I do not mean to advocate that leadership teams should never experience change. I am, however, pointing out an observation that the interdisciplinary divisional leadership teams that saw the most stability during the course of a decade tended to be the best and most consistent performers, particularly in delivering earnings. Certainly there are benefits to ensuring a divisional leadership team has the most talented people possible in every position. However, when it came to empowering a mutual obsession to crush the competition and consistently deliver 20-percent earnings growth, the most stable teams, like the tank crews at NTC and the entire Task Force 4-68, performed the best. Stability, familiarity, and trust in your teammates matter.

All-star sports teams thrown together based on talent alone typically struggle. Greatness may require all-star talent, but only when a group of talented individuals is stabilized and able to bond into a cohesive team over time do they deliver their top performance. Although stability was not often mentioned as one of the core philosophies at Stryker, the best leaders, empowered to deliver 20-percent growth year after year, somehow intuitively understood it and kept their teams stable when they could. At the end of the day, what mattered was performance; and the stable teams that became fully empowered with the organization's obsession tended to deliver.

STABLE VALUES—CODE OF CONDUCT

In addition to personnel stability, John Brown's approach catalyzed a philosophical stability and commonality of thought that greatly empowered people throughout the company. When it came to matters of integrity, Brown once again kept the direction crystal clear through the brevity of his statements.

As he explained, "Over the years I spoke to literally hundreds if not thousands of sales trainees and new people at the company, and one of my lines was that 'they'll have to memorize our conduct manual and that is: Don't lie, don't steal, don't cheat.' And, everybody got that. I really believe it still captures the essence."

The simple rules were like the honor code at West Point, and it was similarly emphasized. There was a zero tolerance policy. At any level, anyone found in clear violation of the rules would be fired no matter how important they may be to the company's efforts. While some may consider such treatment harsh, it was empowering. It was a source of great stability knowing that you worked in an organization that held everyone to the same standard. People would choose the harder *right* over the easier *wrong*.

STABLE VALUES—ENTREPRENEURSHIP

The decentralized structure also brought consistency in how authority and accountability were handled that further served to empower the 20-percent obsession. Stryker people could count on having autonomy. The atmosphere showed a deep understanding of management guru Steven Covey's maxim: "You can't hold someone accountable for results if you supervise their methods." Individual leaders and managers were given great freedom to determine how they were going to do things. The results were what mattered.

At its core, it was a very simple philosophy: Agree on a measurable aggressive goal, hire talented people, give them the resources they need to accomplish the goal, and hold them accountable to the results. The resulting ownership of the goal and the passion people would put toward achieving it drove the company forward.

In 1985's annual report, Brown wrote, "Our decentralized approach permits both the company and the individual employees to understand and measure the contribution of each man and woman in our workforce. We consider this to be an invaluable factor in the financial record of the last nine years."

The great challenge with maintaining such a simple philosophy while a company grows is that it is not simple to keep it so simple. The long and steady tug of bureaucracy constantly arises. Bureaucracies seldom start with an intention to create a quagmire of rules and regulations. They begin as highly responsible people attempt to put checks and balances in a system, usually to ensure the bad thing that just happened doesn't happen again. It all makes sense in the middle of the crisis. After twenty years of adding oversight, developing approval processes, and incorporating more checks and balances, good and well-intentioned people can create miles of red tape. Stryker was exceptional at keeping it simple and keeping the bureaucracy to a minimum.

In the 1992 annual report, as the company was just about to enter the Fortune 500, John Brown wrote a determined note to emphasize that the values and approach of the company would remain constant even as it grew to substantial size.

"Our company's continuing growth," Brown wrote, "presents us with new challenges, but we are well prepared to meet them. As Stryker grows larger, our decentralized structure helps maintain our energy and focus at levels generally found in small, entrepreneurial firms. It appears likely that in 1993, Stryker will, for the first time, find itself listed as a Fortune 500 company. Passing this milestone will reconfirm that Stryker has the critical mass to compete successfully in global markets. But it will in no way diminish our entrepreneurial drive or our long-term objective of 20-percent annual growth in earnings."

Brown was always conscious of how central control could sap the energy of the employee's spirit.

STABLE VALUES — SERVICE ETHIC

Another stable philosophy driving the empowered obsession was an ultrahigh service ethic. Continuous growth requires keeping customers happy. It was difficult enough to find 20 percent more new customers; no sales rep or division could afford to lose customers they had already gained. Accordingly, employees at all levels had the authority to take just about any reasonable action to meet customer needs. Eventually whole departments emerged with responsibilities to keep customers happy and engaged.

In the early days, we had no such luxury. People in R&D, engineering, quality assurance, shipping and receiving, sales, marketing, customer service, and just about every department might become the point person for a customer or a sales rep issue. People knew that they could and usually should drop what they were doing and devote their energy to addressing such an issue. They took care of most problems before leadership became involved. As a project manager for new product programs in my first few years, I would frequently travel to hospital sites to address issues. There was no approval process for these trips, no higher-level sign-off required. If I felt it important to hear firsthand whether customers were having any issues as they began to use our initial production run products, I would go.

The stability provided through the consistency in the corporate leadership team, the simple rules of conduct, and the unwavering decentralization of problem solving served to build mutual ownership in the 20-percent mantra. When your team was delivering 20 percent, the opportunities seemed boundless. Performing teams could open new markets, pursue interesting acquisitions, and experiment with new ideas with nearly complete independent discretion. This freedom (or its lack, in the case of Medical Division during the late 1990s) bonded the teams closely together. It fostered ties at a much lower level, but similar to those reported by soldiers who have been in combat together.

17

YOU AND YOUR

TEAM MATTER

Human organizations tap certain magical powers once they start a streak of success. Over time, a streak alters the collective comfort zone. It gains momentum. The streak evolves from something the organization's members want, to something they expect of themselves, to something they require. Like the flywheel, or the proverbial snowball rolling down a hill, each success builds on the previous wins, and the laws of physics keep the snowball growing larger and larger. A sense of identity develops around the streak, and people will go to extraordinary lengths to keep it alive. For those great coaches and leaders in charge of these organizations, building such a dynasty is a very deliberate act of leadership.

Stryker went public in 1979, and in the very first annual report John Brown clearly stated the company's purpose: "Our goal is to increase sales through the development or acquisition of new products so as to maintain a level of earnings growth in excess of 20 percent a year."

At that point, the company had achieved 20-percent growth for three years in a row. Each year's report would highlight the prior year's accomplishment, note the number of years over which the company had achieved it, and set the continued expectation for 20-percent growth in the year to come.

In the 1981 report, the president's letter noted, "Five years ago, we set two broad goals. One to increase sales through development and acquisition so as to maintain a level of earnings growth in excess of 20 percent a year."

In the 1984 report, the commitment was even more direct: "We can assure you the men and women of Stryker will devote their individual and collective determination to making 1985 nine in a row!" It almost sounds like Fred Dibella.

As the streak continued, it captured the hearts and minds of Stryker's employee base. It became a matter of great pride that the company had met its goal so many years in a row. As you'll remember, Stryker's employees spread the obsession to their friends and family, and the local Kalamazoo paper frequently highlighted Stryker's growth record, spreading it to the community. Success builds on success, and the streak of success at Stryker created a powerful energy to keep it alive. This expectation served to further empower the employee base to achieve it. Most would feel extreme discomfort if ever the streak was in jeopardy.

ALL FOR ONE—RALLYING

Deliberate planning for 20 percent every quarter and every year required a disciplined cadence inside the corporation. Each month and every quarter, the divisions would deliver their projections for the upcoming financial results. As the projections rolled in, John Brown and the CFO would ensure they added to at least 20-percent earnings growth. They would typically maintain a hedge at the corporate level as insurance if any of the divisions failed to meet projected results. If the total was not enough, they would task selected divisions to deliver more.

Occasionally, events inside a division would jeopardize their projection. Orders might not come in as expected, an important product could be put on hold for quality assurance, a large delivery might get canceled or pushed out, supplier issues might mean shortages of a critical part, machinery might break down, or other difficulties could arise. The division would pour every energy into solving the issues. However, sometimes the problems were too significant and a division would have to report their expected shortfall to Corporate. In most instances, the corporate hedge would be able to cover the shortfall; but every once in a while, Corporate would seek additional earnings from the other divisions.

An all-points bulletin would go out, warning that the streak was in jeopardy. In every such instance, the passion to keep the 20-percent streak going drove extraordinary measures. These fiercely competitive divisions would come together and make up the difference. Over twenty-eight years, the divisions rallied together every time it was necessary.

The commitment to keep the streak alive unleashed a primal energy. Individual employees would go to great lengths, as if the long-term reputation of the entire company was on their shoulders. Once, a quality inspector worked thirty-six hours straight to ensure that every product that met requirements was shipped. Shipping worked diligently until midnight to ensure that everything went out within the quarter. Parts buyers drove sixteen-hour round-trips to pick up essential parts. Assemblers worked Saturday and Sunday and every day for a month to meet production demands. Each employee knew that their individual contribution and their extraordinary efforts could make the difference in maintaining the streak.

ONE FOR ALL—HUMILITY

In 1998, the Medical Division team was about halfway through a financial review when Brown's assistant came into the room and whispered an important message to him. We found out later that he had received a consequential and urgent call from the investment bankers regarding the multimillion-dollar Howmedica acquisition. It was absolutely essential that he talk with the bankers about an action that could determine the fate of the company for the next several years. Yet before he left the room, he sincerely apologized for having to interrupt our monthly review and asked that we carry on without him.

The apology and tone left us briefly speechless. It left the impression that he felt our time was important—more important than his own. That kind of humility and care for the time of others from someone in the CEO seat does not happen frequently. Actions like this amplified his influence and ability to empower others. Brown told us with his behavior that our time mattered, and what we did mattered.

DECENTRALIZATION DRIVES OWNERSHIP

Much of Stryker's success can be attributed to driving autonomy down to the lowest level so that everyone felt accountable to the goal. Many organizations attempt to follow a similar approach, and they are able to do it successfully for a year or two. The difference at Stryker was that the high level of personal ownership we all felt inside the divisions did not change as the organization grew from $17 million to over $4 billion in sales. The employees at Stryker felt that their actions mattered, that they were important contributors to achieving the purpose.

You might expect that complacency would begin to gnaw away at the roots of success and threaten to break up the snowball. Indeed, this happens in many organizations, but there was no noticeable sign of contentment within Stryker. Continuous 20-percent growth challenged every division, and working to achieve it left little room for complacency. It was also a goal not just for the year but for every quarter, every month; the pressure never let up. The leaders and managers were constantly concerned over how they would top this year's numbers next year. Celebrations were frequent but brief as the realization that next year you or your team would have to do 20 percent more than the great achievement you were just celebrating.

The intense drive for focus through decentralization was a crucial element in emphasizing the philosophy that each individual's actions would make a difference, that their livelihood was primarily dependent on their personal actions. It drove a sense of ownership and responsibility at every level. The corporate office did not put up obstacles. The entire structure was set up to provide the divisions the resources they needed to overcome the obstacles.

The 2003 annual report noted, "Accountability is a Stryker hallmark. Within the company, cross-functional and intradivisional teams are reinforced by a commitment to individual responsibility, and we employ sophisticated metrics to ensure the reliability of our manufacturing, distribution, and service."

Although many companies tout similar ideals, within Stryker it was universally true. The themes were constant: 20-percent growth, a decentralized organization designed to incite entrepreneurial spirit empowering the obsession to achieve that growth, and a high level of personal and team accountability. Stryker's structure and approach to business captured the energy and enthusiasm found in start-up companies and channeled it into a constant desire to grow.

John Brown's life experiences may have driven his extreme commitment to decentralization. He did not typically talk about himself, so we were all somewhat surprised when he opened up at a company leadership seminar. He told a story that seems harsh in today's world but taught him a valuable and transformative lesson that stayed with him for the rest of his life.

One time when Brown was a young boy, his father and a group of farmhands were busy working to beat an impending thunderstorm and complete a labor-intensive task. Brown was too small at the time to be of much assistance, but he wanted to help. Three times he got in the way of the men working. The first two times, his father scolded him and told him to stay out of the way. On the third time, Brown described a rubber hose coming across his face and an order along the lines of "I won't tell you again."

Despite the painful experience, Brown described the immensely valuable lesson he learned: "When people are working hard, stay out of their way." A successful farm requires people able to stay focused on their tasks. In the face of impending weather, every hand knows that what they are doing could make or break the year's crop. Likewise, Stryker's decentralized structure ensured that corporate headquarters stayed out of the way of those divisions delivering their numbers.

A PERSONAL PUSH

Just as the start-up EMS team was introducing our new RUGGED stretcher and finishing preparations for initial production and shipments, the situation at Patient Care had become dire. The cost of the bed was a mission-critical problem, and solving it would require extreme measures. Early in my Stryker career, I had led teams to great success in design cost optimization, manufacturing cost reduction, and product quality improvement. If a similar transformation could happen with the new medical–surgical bed, the cost problem would be solved. Pursuant to this idea, Harry Carmitchel (Medical Division president) and Brown concluded that it would be necessary to transfer me to the Patient Care division. Needless to say, joining Pickett's Charge was not on the top of my list of things to do. It would have been easy for Carmitchel to simply call me into his office and tell me I had been reassigned. I would have started at Patient Care the next week as ordered, but such a technique would not likely have captured my heart nor further inspired a maniacal obsession to achieve the mission.

Instead, Brown met with me in his corner office at the building by the airport. The conversation was short, cordial, and focused. Wrapping it up, Brown said something along the lines of "I would like you to go into that office next door and think about it, then call Harry and let him know whether you will be joining Patient Care."

I knew there was no decision to be made. The CEO was asking me to take a new assignment. I had to do it, but part of me felt as if I was being forced back into that cross-attached unit for the first NTC rotation.

As I sat down in the adjoining office, next to the phone was one of those multiphoto wooden frames. At the bottom was an engraving that read *Stryker's Champions of Innovation.* In the frame were pictures of Dr. Stryker, William Chang (VP of R&D for Endoscopy), Jim Evans (VP of R&D for Instruments), and two of the ingenious R&D and science leaders from Osteonics.

In the last frame was my picture.

Being grouped with these incredible engineers and scientists was both humbling and inspiring. I was hooked and made the call to Carmitchel immediately. John Brown knew that truly engaging people is not about commanding them to do something; it is about getting them to command themselves to do it.

SELLING AUTONOMY

This atmosphere served to attract the kind of people who were looking for a challenge and wanted their work to matter. If I reached the point in an interview for a design engineer where a candidate was clearly someone we wanted, I would shift from asking questions evaluating the candidate into trying to sell the company to the candidate.

We would talk about the environment at Stryker. The typical opening was, "This is really the best of both worlds from a company-size point of view. We have the resources of a substantial corporation, but at the same time we have the focus, intensity, and intimacy of a small business. All of the action is happening in the divisions. The corporate office is small. It's John Brown, the CFO, a general counsel, and a bunch of accountants. That's it. The balance sheet is loaded with cash, and they're looking for the right investments to make. Corporate is the best bank in the world, and the divisions are expected to bring the ideas that will drive 20-percent growth."

I would attempt a contrast with other opportunities in which the candidate might be interested, particularly with new graduates: "You know, you can join one of the big three auto firms"—we were in Michigan, after all—"or their suppliers, and that would be a great gig. You'll have a large team of talented engineers around you to learn from. You'll have a well-defined structure, with career paths pretty clearly detailed and extensive training plans and resources. And on your first day at work, they will hand you a tool for you to use in your first few years; it will be a jeweler's screwdriver. You may be on the steering column team, and you'll tweak this part of the design here and improve it over there; three to five years from now you'll see the fruits of your labor in a new vehicle design.

"But we're not like that," I'd continue. "We always have more work that needs to be done than we have people to do it. So we'll hand you a tool on your first day, and it will be a sledgehammer. You'll become part of a small, focused team with broad responsibilities for the design of an entirely new product. You'll be stretched and pulled in many different directions, you'll be given more latitude than you can imagine, and in about eighteen to twenty-four months we'll launch the product that your team designed. It will be something that customers love and sales reps are clamoring to get their hands on to sell."

We wanted the kind of engineer who would be inspired and not intimidated by this description, those who wanted their work to matter and had a burning desire to make a difference.

John Brown orchestrated Stryker's environment to ensure that people at every level understood their individual contribution toward the 20-percent goal mattered. Much like 4-68's soldiers under the playbook concept, the actions of just a few could have a profound impact on the larger organization. The drive to keep our 20-percent streak alive often inspired heroic actions.

18

AFFECTING LIVES
AND CAREERS
AT STRYKER

A saying often heard at the sales awards ceremonies, the Chairman's Breakfast, and other celebratory events was that "Stryker is a place where dreams are made." It speaks to the impact that working in the company had on many people. The high autonomy–high responsibility environment set amid a backdrop of constant growth allowed opportunities for personal and professional success far exceeding those in a typical business. Growth in the business was highly aligned with growth in the professional lives of those within it. The chance to do more, to make even greater contributions, to build new or larger teams, to be a part of something thriving and expanding was uplifting and inspiring. The constant addition of new product lines, new sales regions, new production lines, new manufacturing plants, new supervisors, managers, directors, and vice presidents—even entire new divisions—created incredible opportunities for people in the company.

ENRICHING LIVES

Reflecting on the impact working at Stryker had on his life, one top-performing sales rep told a story at an awards ceremony that I will do my best to paraphrase:

"I was down on my luck, and we had moved in with the in-laws due to a shortage of funds. We literally did not have enough for food and shelter.

"Then the initial interviews happened with Stryker. I became enthralled with the company, the products I would sell, the people I would work with, and the straight-commission opportunity. Even before receiving an offer or attending my final interviews in Kalamazoo, I piled my wife and kids into the car. We drove out to the exclusive neighborhood in town. I pointed to a beautiful home and said, 'Something incredible is happening. I know I am going to work for Stryker, and it is going to change our lives. We are going to live in a house like that and have all the things we only dream of today.'"

This rep would join the Medical Division and go on to become one of the most respected reps in the company. His annual compensation would occasionally exceed that of Mr. Brown. Fulfilling his own prophecy, he would buy a huge home in that neighborhood, and the lives of his family were forever improved.

A job at Stryker marked a turning point in many people's professional and personal lives. People would join as assembly-line workers and launch into a career that would eventually see them in charge of an entire factory. Creative people would join as shop technicians and work their way into new jobs and new experiences. One person joined in the R&D shop, went on to get a BA from the local university, and eventually was put in charge of international marketing for an entire division. The R&D leader for the EMS team literally got his start sweeping the sidewalks in front of the original building; years later, he led immensely creative teams that won 20 percent of the corporation's overall R&D awards. Many division presidents started as sales reps, moved into marketing or sales management, and eventually ended up leading entire businesses. It was a place where hard work, ingenuity, intelligence, and a burning ambition to be successful paid amazing personal and professional dividends.

CREATING WEALTH

Although the compensation opportunities for people outside the sales team were not nearly as great, with constant growth, Brown capitalized on other tools to build deep alignment with the obsession for 20-percent growth. The company's 401(k) program was best in class. Those who contributed 8 percent of their income toward it would see a total equaling 19 percent of their pretax income going toward their personal retirement plan every year. Once Stryker became publicly traded, Brown and the board immediately started a key employee stock-option program. Although this is common in the entrepreneurial arena of Silicon Valley, such a move was quite unusual in the staid manufacturing state of Michigan. Like its Silicon Valley counterparts, the option program's goals were rewarding and recognizing exceptional contributions, recruiting top talent, and retaining key employees. Over many years it was an important factor in empowering the 20-percent obsession. Few things build personal ownership for an organization's goals as well as an equity stake in the company. With Stryker's 20-percent earnings growth having such a clear and visible connection to the stock price, this building of personal wealth was a powerful influence for many key employees.

The magic of compound returns worked wonders for what may initially have seemed a small option grant. For example, an option grant of 1,000 shares would be worth nothing on the day it was bestowed. It would, however, be controlling what was usually about $30 per share, or

$30,000 of stock. If the share price rose above $30, any increase would be a gain for the option holder. If the stock price did not appreciate, there would be no benefit; but this was a company growing earnings by 20 percent or more per year. Stryker's typical stock market returns would make such a 1,000-share grant worth nearly $250,000 by the tenth year. Given the consistent and exceptional market returns, key contributors such as engineers who devised significant innovations, high-performing managers in sales or other departments, and other successful divisional leaders could have $100,000 to more than $1,000,000 in outstanding option value accruing at least 20 percent per year at any given time. For an engineer in the state of Michigan at the time, this was a powerful incentive.

The option program was something Brown kept very close to his vest. For many years, Brown and the option committee made the final decisions regarding who the recipients would be and the number of shares they would receive. They would get recommendations from the division presidents, but the ultimate decision and authority rested with Brown. It was his method to ensure that the options were not a popularity contest. Those who contributed most clearly to the 20-percent earnings growth would receive the grants. There was no entitlement; it was based solely on performance.

Brown would handwrite a personal note to each awardee, expressing gratitude for their work and typically setting expectations for more great contributions ahead. It was a powerful motivator. Although the successful salespeople were the most highly paid employees of the company, they were not typically included in the stock-option program. For long-term employees, it was often said that the highest paid folks were in sales, but the most wealthy were engineers and other home-office people who had held on to their stock and stock options over the long haul.

The option committee sent a standard letter to each option grantee, expressing that the options were "not intended to be used as supplemental income." It explained that the options were an instrument to align the key employee's personal financial interests with those of the company, to recognize contributions, and to inspire more extraordinary efforts toward the long-term goal of at least 20-percent earnings growth per year.

Stryker executives seldom emulated the behavior of many top executives in public companies today. Top-employee stock-option exercises are required to be reported to the Securities and Exchange Commission (SEC), and I am always a bit disheartened to see the exercise of an option and the immediate sale of all the shares. This behavior is common and tolerated at many great firms, particularly those in Silicon Valley. At Stryker, such behavior would be frowned on and might even be a reason to limit your option grants in the future. The equity was intended to drive loyalty and align financial interests. It was perfectly acceptable to sell whatever number of shares was needed to satisfy tax obligations, but the expectation beyond that was that you would retain the shares and build your personal wealth in the company. With the stock price typically growing at more than 20 percent per year it was generally a wise financial decision to keep them.

With nostalgic overtones during our 2015 conversation Brown spoke about the impact he believed the company had on employees' lives: "When I stepped down, we had 50,000–60,000 people. I'll tell you, at least 10,000 of them I know really endorsed the Stryker 20-percent profit goal, because they were all benefiting from it. Their jobs were firm, stable; they got increases; many of them got equity. And so everybody was doing well financially and doing well emotionally. Everything was just heading in the right direction."

Brown capitalized on the many tools available in a free enterprise to aid in inspiring loyalty and spreading the obsession.

The best corporate leaders create unique environments that entice members of their organizations to feel that they are part of something special, something genuine, and most important—something worth their absolute best. They work tirelessly to ensure the success of the business and the success of those within it. They delight in celebrating the accomplishments of others. They build organizations that leave a lasting and positive impact on the lives of those who join. John Brown influenced thousands to acquire an obsession with growth and to build a career in an organization that was constantly evolving. Over twenty-eight years, the lives of tens of thousands of people—and those of their families—were changed by Brown's leadership. In the process, the majority identified with the omnipresent goal of 20-percent growth and worked with an obsessive passion to achieve it.

PART 3

UNLEASHING CREATIVITY

In a sense, providing absolute clarity and empowering an obsession to go 9–0 at NTC or achieve 20-percent earnings growth every year enabled the most cogent of the three magical metathemes—unleashing creativity. Achieving extreme levels of performance required relentless innovation in multiple parts of the organization, all at the same time. Ingenuity and creativity flourished; they were the source of the dramatic improvements in everyday functions within these organizations that allowed them to realize their purpose. The thirst for better ways of doing things was deeply interwoven into the organizational mindset. Like the explosion of innovation that arose during World War II when entire nations were obsessed with winning the war, creative minds in every part of these organizations focused extreme levels of energy on developing new technologies, processes, and methods that would enable achieving the purpose.

These creative environments were not like artistic, open-thought communities or undirected research labs; the innovation was supremely purposeful. Neither Stryker nor Task Force 4-68 was looking for fashionable ideas that would lead to immediate but only short-term gains. Stryker's focus was on products, services, and enabling processes on which a lasting business could be built over many years; and 4-68 developed the playbook and its battle plans to win every maneuver battle every time. New ideas had to contribute to that overall goal. Consultants who studied Stryker in the late 1990s termed it *innovation that endures*.

Unleashing creativity brought about thousands of little innovations that were the crucial catalysts in delivering exceptional results. In both organizations, challenging the status quo, inventing new methods, envisioning better ways to do things, and devising new and improved processes or procedures were encouraged at all levels. Those ideas that resulted in significant advances were highly lauded and praised, especially from the top.

Once again, the influence of the top leaders was remarkably similar. Fred Dibella was out front, voraciously collecting ideas, asking for input, and driving the refinement of the playbook and other procedures across the task force. John Brown constantly pushed and prodded for new ideas and improvements throughout the company. He was a primary catalyst for spreading the stories of success company-wide. He was also actively involved with the hiring for R&D leadership in every division. There were common expectations and enabling patterns of behavior that you could count on inside either organization. Three consistent elements describe the similar influence in unleashing creative energies.

First, through their personal involvement, these leaders created environments of direct, honest, and open communication that elevated ideas on the basis of their merits. Challenging the status quo was permitted and even encouraged, and the top leader set the example. Ideas were celebrated and shared, and their inventors were recognized and rewarded. The evaluation criteria were also simple and objective, summed up in a statement heard from multiple leaders in both organizations: "If it works, do it."

Second, the champions of ideas could find resources for experimentation to validate or invalidate ideas. This is not to say that there was some magical pool of assets available to go after every idea. There was not. Time, money, and other needed resources were precious commodities, and for an idea to obtain those resources it had to have champions. The effort to secure crucial assets or their scarcity typically strengthened the resolve to make the ideas work. It also weeded out those with lukewarm commitments. There was high accountability for the champions but also a high tolerance for failure. This seemingly contradictory ethos was clearer than it sounds. Both leaders exhibited a considerable understanding for mistakes of the mind but little for mistakes of the heart.

Third, they established a pervasive organizational mindset in which the organization's members at all levels worked to constantly improve. Many of the most important innovations arose out of the relentless energy poured into making systems, processes, or products just a little better every day. Incremental gains every day, every week, and every month in primary support systems compounded over time and led to dramatic systemic improvements. In many cases, these highly evolved systems gave the organizations fundamental advantages. All of these were key facilitators of the extraordinary results.

19

PURPOSE-DRIVEN CREATIVITY IN TASK FORCE 4-68

Developing highly effective new ways to conduct combined arms combat operations was essential to the success of 4-68. The thirst for new ideas and better ways of doing things was as deeply interwoven into the unit's psyche as the obsession with conquering the OPFOR and the clarity of that purpose. Embracing ingenuity was the third leg of our stool of success. Clarity of purpose defined our reason to exist, empowering the obsession spread the passion to achieve, and obsessive pursuit of the goal led to high levels of performance from every member of the team; but it was unleashed creativity that made it all possible. The innovations this team developed were remarkable.

Given the short time frame of the lead-up to the NTC, 4-68's history provides a striking case study of how unleashing people's innate creative spirit can rapidly transform an organization's performance. A maverick, unafraid to challenge ingrained dogma, Dibella would inspire the team to brainstorm, develop, and embrace new and more efficient methods. What mattered was not where the ideas came from but how effective they might be in improving our combat effectiveness.

Convinced that defeating the OPFOR in all nine battles would require ingenuity at every level, he made it not just acceptable but essential to challenge conventional wisdom. In his auditorium presentation of the 9–0 objective, he bluntly acknowledged that the OPFOR was destroying task forces that religiously followed Army doctrine. He challenged us to do things differently. His willingness to bet on a completely new concept for devising and executing our battle plans—a simplified playbook of tactics patterned after the wishbone offense—made it clear to the officers and enlisted personnel that he embraced creative approaches.

The fact that our commander championed an unorthodox idea entailing a radically different approach to the core elements of conducting combat operations had far-reaching effects. Following suit, the subsequent engagement in constructing and refining the plays unleashed soldiers at every level from the confines of Army doctrine. Ingenuity was essential, and Fred Dibella became its greatest catalyst.

THE PLAYBOOK WAS MORE THAN A DOCUMENT

The NTC veterans knew that going out to California expecting to do a few things better than other task forces would not crack the OPFOR's formidable armor. TF 4-68 would have to plan and execute appreciably better in all seven of the combat operating systems to have any chance at winning every battle. The playbook was a critical enabler, and for all the reasons previously mentioned, it contributed substantially to our results. But many have inaccurately pointed to the playbook and the intricacies of the plays themselves as the key.

Following our rotation, many young commanders attempted to take the plays as a cookie-cutter technique to fighting battles, but the essence of what made the playbook work was lost in this approach. It was the collaborative process of developing the plays that mattered most—the continuous reevaluation, tweaking, and retweaking, and the entire team's engagement in developing this innovative approach—that made the playbook so powerful. The document codified the collective ideas of the task force's soldiers, but the actual collection of ideas was more than we could put onto paper. The playbook itself was, in a sense, an extension of our collective mind.

In developing it, we became voracious learners and experimenters looking to gain every insight from those who had been through NTC rotations and to try out new approaches with every training exercise. In our one-year lead-up period to the NTC, we saw an explosion of ingenuity and new methods more prolific than most organizations experience in a decade. Developing the playbook unleashed the creative drive in every aspect of task-force operations. The point was to win, to use our ingenuity and the understanding of our strengths and weaknesses to seek every advantage we could. TF 4-68 challenged conventional wisdom on nearly every front; we had to revamp, reshape, refine, and reinvent nearly every element of combat execution. For every facet—the concept of the operation, the command and control, the communication techniques, the organizational approach, the service and support—4-68 devised new ways of getting things done.

This commitment to innovate was especially remarkable in the backdrop of the US military at the time. It is rare for the last major war's victor to develop new methodologies for fighting. Although the US Army had many things called into question following the debacle of Vietnam, that was not a large-scale-maneuver war. By the mid 1980s, the country had been fighting the Cold War for three decades. Hard-fought lessons from World War II had become cemented into doctrine. The lessons learned in the bloody mountains of North Africa, the difficult terrain of Sicily and Italy, and the hedgehog-strewn plains of northern France were valuable but needed updating. The army had built a large amount of organizational inertia around what had worked in our last major maneuver war. Moreover, an environment such as the military, where discipline and the requirement to follow orders are drilled into soldiers from the very first day, is not typically considered a hotbed for innovation. 4-68 was the opposite of that staid military stereotype.

Dibella used his personal charisma to fan the creative fires, starting with his first presentations to the task force. His actions then reinforced his words. A creative firestorm began with that very first simulated battle and the smoke screen confrontation with our brigade observer. That encounter and many subsequent ones built a galvanizing level of trust within the unit. A trust that new ideas were welcome became transformational.

Dibella cultivated a culture of selflessness, a willingness to risk our lives as any soldier does, but also to risk our careers to meet a higher goal. There was no patience for politics. Considerations of career advancement in the day-to-day business of leading soldiers and getting us combat ready would be counterproductive. In the command environment of many units, genuinely creative brainstorming and experimentation required putting your reputation on the line. If you tried something against doctrine, and it did not work out, the career consequences would be harsh. Dibella turned that model upside down.

As he related later, "The only way to get us to the level needed to beat the OPFOR was to take extreme risk, to try new things, to fail and fail again, but to always strive. Sadly, in the conventional Officer Efficiency Report (OER) system, that kind of behavior is not often rewarded because it entails a bit of maverick mentality. So you had to trust your rater to take care of you and focus only on getting better and better."

Mark Pires, a former captain in the battalion staff, noted the impact of Dibella's approach: "He pulled everyone in in a way that was collaborative in terms of how we were going to do it. He had a great way of establishing an open environment, where people understood they could make mistakes. So you were able to take some risk. It was the tone he set not just by his words but by his actions. You saw that when people made mistakes, they weren't getting their knees cut off."

Nearly every officer and NCO of 4-68 can describe a personal story of how their own ideas became incorporated into the fabric of 4-68. The playbook codified this fabric and encapsulated the collective wisdom of sergeants, captains, lieutenants, and other soldiers throughout the task force and its support units. It takes a special environment to ensure that ideas surface and that the best ideas win. Under Dibella, the embrace of ingenuity was everywhere.

SENDING ONE OF OUR OWN TO NTC

When I joined the Alpha Company, the Army bestowed me with a great deal more responsibility than I had the wisdom or experience to be reasonably given, as they often do with new lieutenants. Although I was green and untested, I was an eager and quick learner. With the assistance of an exceptional group of NCOs, I started to discover how to actually lead a maneuver unit. The Army's training, along with an impassioned study of military history, had filled my mind with myriad tools and techniques for leadership and battle. Applying this knowledge in actual situations was a very different challenge.

After about two months of stumbling through several simulated operations, the platoon's NCOs had at least helped develop my skills to the point where I could handle two radio networks (tank internal and company command nets) blaring through my helmet, direct my own tank, keep track of my platoon's tanks on the battlefield, navigate the terrain, and issue commands once the enemy engaged. This is when Dibella picked my platoon for the fortuitous cross-attachment mission with the other battalion. This mission allowed me to help 4-68 in ways I would have never thought possible.

Dibella later revealed to me that "Dave Carruthers and I specifically selected you because we knew that when you returned, you would be the single best man to impart lessons learned—and we were right."

We will call this unit 1-17 Armor for simplicity. Although it was an outstanding opportunity from a military-training standpoint, some of my soldiers were not overjoyed at the prospects of six weeks of intensive field preparations and then the monthlong experience in the Mojave Desert. We also became part of a unit where we were the new kids on the block and did not know the other soldiers or commanders. Nonetheless, we set out to make the best of it. Dibella sold it as a great opportunity for 4-68. An indigenous tank platoon would learn the terrain at NTC and gain valuable experience against the OPFOR. Little did I know all the ways he would ensure the task force capitalized on what we learned.

The tank company we were attached to had two other tank platoons with competent, seasoned platoon leaders and a strong cadre of NCOs. I absorbed a great deal from them. That company commander was also a solid leader, and I looked forward to working with him. However, when it came to the actual maneuver battles, my platoon usually ended up being further cross-attached to an infantry company.

The infantry company commander, Captain Moranis, displayed a temperament on the radio net in the middle of intense battles much like that of Attila the Hun. The command environment in 1-17 was generally consistent with that of average units in the Army. They were serious about their training exercises and approached simulated combat with determination. They developed optimized plans for each battle using the tools and techniques leaders were taught in training courses. They placed strong emphasis on solid execution and supporting each other during the Multiple Integrated Laser Engagement System or MILES-simulated combat exercises.

FACING THE CARNAGE

The NTC rotation for 1-17 was a typical one for an American unit. We won only two of the nine battles, and it seemed like the OPFOR offered a gimme for the final offensive engagement, in which we massively outnumbered the defenders. During the course of the rotation, I had the chance to strike up a relationship with one of the senior

Observer–Controllers (OCs), a seasoned lieutenant colonel with several years' experience at the NTC. He had spent significant time with Captain Moranis's company. The OC had seen the OPFOR chew up unit after unit over the past eighteen months and was understandably more than a bit cynical about the competence of the American commanders. I was genuinely grateful that he did not feel it was a waste of his time to share his insights with a green second lieutenant from another battalion. Captain Moranis was consumed with other responsibilities and was understandably a bit aloof from the OC, who was his evaluator for the rotation.

The OC could foretell with nearly supernatural prescience what would happen in many of the battles. At dusk one evening, while we were preparing for a defensive operation, he climbed onto my tank. We sat on the turret in the waning desert heat as the sky slowly darkened. He discussed the upcoming battle, as it was likely to unfold:

"Scouts will come out tonight and pinpoint the location of every tank, every infantry platoon, and every minefield. They will silently clear a path through the minefields, probably here and here," he said, pointing to locations on the terrain map. "A small group of tanks will make a demonstration somewhere to the north, and when your battalion command becomes convinced this decoy is the main assault, they'll deploy assets to stop it. That is when the real operation will start. The main body will come straight down this dry wadi. The OPFOR call it the *Colorado River*, referring to its size. Its flat bottom facilitates fast traffic, and its steep sides offer defilade from enemy fire. The mines and obstacles you've set up to block access will all be cleared before the assault begins. They'll flank the rest of the battalion and be in your rear areas within an hour."

This is exactly what happened.

The OPFOR went through 1-17 the next morning, as General George S. Patton would say, "like crap through a goose." Within an hour after the first shots were fired, OPFOR tanks and personnel carriers were raiding 1-17's rear area and supply lines. Some OPFOR elements turned around to shoot and kill our remaining tanks from behind. 1-17's defense was completely ineffective. My platoon had the opportunity to fire only a few shots as we moved to a vantage point from which we could see into the wadi and engage the fast-moving OPFOR elements. However, the OPFOR focused on the limited remaining resistance and employed their fire support elements to eliminate it. An OC came over to my tank and asked me to engage the MILES kill light, because we had been destroyed by enemy artillery fire.

Following the After-Action Review, Captain Moranis said the OPFOR scouts knew the position of every minefield and every dug-in position by the early morning. OPFOR artillery, air, or recon patrols took positions that offered good fire into the wadi they used as their axis of attack. They penetrated right into our softened underbelly. In an actual war, 1-17 would have been completely cut off and then starved into surrender. I was beginning to understand the OPFOR's invincibility.

A few days later, the entire brigade's offensive operation had an even more horrific end. 1-17 was the follow-on battalion in what was planned as a two-stage brigade coordinated attack. When they reached the first intermediate objective, our sister battalion would hand off the primary offensive to 1-17. Our objective lay at the top of a bowl-shaped expanse of terrain in Fort Irwin's maneuver area known as *Siberia*. The objective for 1-17 was about five kilometers farther along the same axis as the sister battalion's intermediate objective.

For this operation, my platoon went back to its parent tank company. The tank company's mission was simple: We were to hold the left flank of the battalion's position while the sister battalion took control of the intermediate objective. Following that, we would move along the left flank and provide overwatch support for 1-17's advance to the final objective. My platoon was to be the farthest to the left.

The operation unfolded very differently from the plan.

My platoon's vantage point as we bounded up the side of the bowl gave us spectacular views of the battle shaping up to our right. We watched as the vanguard elements of the main attack met their first resistance. A few puffs of smoke to the right of the main column, and the kill lights for the battalion's lead tanks lit up. More puffs of smoke, and five more friendly vehicles were hit. It was at about that point that one of my platoon's tank commanders spotted an enemy tank hiding inside a dug-in position to our front.

We were far from the battalion's main attack. I reported to the company commander, and we proceeded to attack with two tanks overwatching and two advancing. One of our tanks reached a position with a clear line of sight to the enemy tank. They took it out. We were elated to see the kill lights on the OPFOR tanks light. Bounding forward, we spotted three or four other isolated enemy tanks and proceeded to take them out piecemeal. Only one of our tanks was "killed" in the process.

At this point, I looked to see what was happening in the main assault on the intermediate objective. It was a sight that I will never forget. There were more than fifty friendly vehicles with MILES kill lights flashing all along the main avenue of approach. No friendly elements had made it through. To make matters worse, the other companies of 1-17 were rolling full speed down the same avenue of approach toward this kill zone. I got on the radio to warn the commander of what appeared to be a death march for our sister companies. There was no answer. There was no one left on the net.

Scrambling through my Signal Corps codex to find the battalion command frequency, I manually changed stations so my radio could communicate. An assistant operations officer answered. I told him that we were on the left flank and had taken out a platoon of enemy tanks. By this time, our battalion's elements were becoming engaged in the same kill zone. I recommended they deviate to a different approach. He said the intermediate objective had been cleared and ordered me to proceed toward the objective by continuing to flank toward the left. Although I did not fully understand what was happening in the main assault, our battalion seemed likely to suffer the same fate as the first. We were too far away to provide any overwatch for the main element, and I was being ordered to move even farther left.

Maneuvering through small wadis and up the left flank of the bowl-shaped position, we took out a few more enemy vehicles and eventually reached the physical location of the objective, losing only one more tank in the process.

It didn't matter. There were no OPFOR forces in the objective.

From there, I looked back down into the bowl. 1-17 had been slaughtered as efficiently as the lead battalion. Over a hundred MILES lights blinked over the two kilometers of the brigade's main avenue of approach. I was to later learn that five enemy tanks had virtually slaughtered two battalions of American troops. The OPFOR stayed hunkered down in their dugout positions, rising only to shoot as the Americans continued to roll down the avenue of approach, platoon after platoon, company after company, into the slaughter. It was like the Union troops valiantly charging General Thomas Jackson's wall at the First Battle of Bull Run and dying, a battle after which the Confederate general would forever be known as Stonewall Jackson. I remember thinking how horrible the situation would be if this were actual warfare. So many lives would have been lost.

Following this disaster, we began preparations for another defensive engagement. This time my platoon was given an unusual mission. We were initially deployed to the forward-most position as the battalion set up for battle. Our orders were not to dig in but to maintain vigilance, warding off enemy scouts as the remainder of the battalion completed their entrenchments and fortifications. Early in the morning we would then redeploy to a position behind the other elements of the battalion, where we would become a mobile reserve.

Late in the evening, the lieutenant colonel OC stopped by my tank, and we talked for a bit. He told me that one of the big issues in the brigade's attack in *Siberia* had been communications. A critical radio message from the sister battalion to the brigade had been completely misunderstood. Before his tank was taken out, one of the last surviving company commanders in the sister battalion jumped onto the brigade net to warn that the battalion had been decimated. Somehow, this was misconstrued as a notification that the OPFOR had been eliminated from the intermediate objective. 1-17 was then given orders to roll through and begin their attack on the final objective. 1-17's lead elements expected the route to be clear and rolled forward at full travel speed to begin their follow-up attack—right into the kill zone.

We also talked about the unusual nature of my platoon's mission in the upcoming battle. Familiar with how the Germans used similar ideas, having a mobile reserve that could rush to the critical area to slow the advance of the Russian army in the latter years of World War II, we both thought this was an interesting concept. But he warned me about our counterrecon role.

"You'll have to keep a sharp eye out for the enemy scouts," he said. "They know this terrain and all its hidden passes and places to hide. They'll be tough to spot. Traveling back through the battalion's position will also be a lot more difficult at 5:00 in the morning than it sounds. Make sure you know the route."

Once again, the OC was prescient. At about 3:00 a.m., one of my platoon's tank crews spotted some movement to our left front. I swung my turret around and, looking through the thermal sights, could see the antenna of an OPFOR reconnaissance vehicle moving through the desert brush about 1500 meters to our front. Relaying the information to battalion headquarters, they asked if we had a clear shot. None of our tanks could see more than the enemy antennas and an occasional glimpse of its turret. Battalion decided to dispatch elements of our scout platoon to engage this enemy. We spotted no further activity for the remainder of our watch.

At 5:00 a.m., we started the maneuver to our rearward position. It was tedious; the movement should have taken about twenty minutes, but it was a good hour before we finally reached the rear position. One tank's track broke while traveling through a rocky wadi, and it took time to fix. Captain Moranis was little help as he screamed profanities over the company command net deriding our slow progress. Nonetheless, we reached the position, behind a large outcropping that completely hid us from view along most avenues of approach. Relieved to finally reach our position, we performed basic maintenance and awaited further orders.

The OPFOR columns rolled at sunrise.

Despite the refined defensive plan and counter-reconnaissance during the night, the OPFOR once again seemed to have an intimate knowledge of the battalion's defensive positions. OPFOR reconnaissance forces deep in our position vigorously attacked and destroyed the 1-17 units guarding the main axis of attack. When the main OPFOR columns rolled, they penetrated straight through the American position. We received no order to move for reinforcement; the OPFOR was simply too fast.

The effectiveness of the OPFOR reconnaissance and then the shock and awe of their initial thrust left 1-17 gasping for air. However, the enemy did not know the location of my platoon, because we had moved so early in the morning. The gunner in my tank was first to notice an OPFOR vehicle rolling right past our right side and about 1500 meters away. Suddenly there were two, then three, then dozens. We surmised they had blasted through the battalion's defenses and were headed to the supply trains. Taking a page out of the book we had seen the OPFOR use with devastating effect during the battle in *Siberia*, my platoon turned to the south and started to engage.

The terrain was advantageous. We rolled our tanks back down a slight rise in the southern face, where they would not be seen by the OPFOR column. We could then rise to fire and roll back to cover. As the enemy regiment moved west, we had excellent fields of fire and could engage them from their right side and rear.

MILES kill lights blinked throughout the OPFOR regiment. After more than forty enemy vehicles were killed, OPFOR began to realize where the fire originated. Twenty vehicles turned to attack our position.

Again, the terrain worked to our advantage. We killed several more enemy tanks before the battle turned into a stalemate. After about twenty minutes, OPFOR infantry were dismounting to attempt a ground assault on our position when the OCs called the operation over. Most of the 1-17 had been outflanked and destroyed, and they wanted to get to the After-Action Review before noon. My platoon had killed upwards of fifty vehicles while sustaining no casualties.

This operation taught some valuable lessons that I was eager to share with anyone who would listen. I could go on discussing that first NTC experience with 1-17, but it would not be germane to the topic at hand. The battalion improved as a result of the exercises, and the rotation prepared them for an actual engagement. I had the opportunity to bond with my platoon, and we all looked forward to returning to the Silver Lions.

SHARING OUR EXPERIENCES

When we returned to the battalion, Dibella scheduled a private meeting in his office with me and my platoon sergeant. After the first minute, it was clear he was intensely interested in understanding what we had learned from the NTC experience. I was just a young lieutenant, but he listened as if we had just returned from Jedi training with Master Yoda.

Our meeting lasted far beyond the scheduled time. Toward the end, Dibella insisted that I prepare a presentation and bring my platoon sergeant to the next Officers' Professional Development (OPD) meeting and talk about each of the battles and the takeaways from the experience.

"Everyone has to know these things," he said. "How you saw the OPFOR plan and execute their battles, the things you learned from the OC, the tricks they use to gather intelligence—all of it. They can be beaten, but we have to be very, very smart to do it."

I left the meeting totally engaged and highly enthused.

Dibella set the stage at the OPD meeting and used me to the best of my capabilities. I was a student of military history who spent thousands of hours playing war games when I was younger, which gave me some ability to make sense of the placement of units on a map, much like a chess master makes sense of the interplay of pieces on the board. Dibella seemed to see this in me and, despite our vast differences in rank and actual experience, he listened.

I prepared maps that could be shown on the overhead projector with unit symbols and arrows showing the history of each battle. We discussed every battle in painstaking detail. The playbook concept had not yet been officially rolled out, nor had the 9–0 objective; but the thought processes were under way. All the energy in the room was directed toward figuring out how we could avoid 1-17's fate. Much of what I related reinforced what the others had learned from research on the NTC and from their own experiences.

DISSECTING LESSONS LEARNED POINT BY POINT

The OPFOR's near-complete knowledge of 1-17's defensive schemes along with the intriguing record of my platoon in the second defensive operation, where we took out nearly fifty OPFOR vehicles, sparked considerable discussion. OPFOR counted on the keen accuracy of their reconnaissance elements to pinpoint enemy strongpoints and plan their attack. Repositioning early in the morning could throw off the OPFOR, because their reconnaissance reports would be out of date. From this we developed the decoy positions discussed earlier, where we would position most of our combat elements during the evening prior to a defensive battle while engineers would be preparing our eventual battle positions.

Furthermore, the ineffectiveness of my platoon at spotting and keeping the OPFOR patrols out of 1-17's defensive position, even while using thermal-imaging sights, sparked more discussion. The deep wadis and terrain offered good cover, and the OPFOR patrols were highly familiar with them. The eventual defensive plays would assign an entire mechanized infantry company to keeping the OPFOR reconnaissance out of our positions. Only dismounted infantry could cover the nooks and crannies that the OPFOR used. Even then, we knew some would get in, but we would confuse them with the decoy positions.

After all this lively discussion, Dibella summed up the critical lesson: No matter what else we did, we would have to win the recon–counterrecon war. That was step one. If they knew exactly where we were, they would kill us. This became one of the three primary principles embodied within the playbook.

While discussing the disastrous offensive battle in *Siberia*, two key lessons stood out: First and foremost, communication must be clear, accurate, and concise. An entire battalion had literally charged into an OPFOR kill zone because of a miscommunication. Clarity on the radio and in written orders would become a linchpin in 4-68's operating procedures.

I did not recognize the second lesson until discussing the experiences with the team. If you recall from the earlier story, my platoon had actually reached the final objective. By maneuvering around the flank of the enemy, one platoon of tanks managed to inflict as much or more damage to the OPFOR than two battalions along the main attack route. This idea of hitting the enemy in the flank has been around since the battle of Marathon, when the Persians first invaded Greece in 490 BC. It is one of the fundamental principles of war, and it was to become a second principle of the plays in the *Silver Lions Playbook*.

OPD meetings such as this one, After-Action Reviews, sand-table drills, brown-bag lunches, and everyday conversations unleashed remarkable creativity within the task force. The energy filtered down through the companies into the platoons, then into the tank crews and infantry squads. Nearly everyone became engaged in developing, experimenting, and finding new and better ways to do things.

DOING OUR HOMEWORK

Years later, Dibella would reflect back on these important elements of the development process.

He said, "One of the things we perpetually did in 4-68 in the process

of playbook development was our *homework*. I would take several officers from the staff or line companies to every maneuver unit who had
just returned to Carson from the NTC, and we would interview their
commanders and operators to get real-time lessons learned. We spoke
to colonels, captains, and sergeants. They all had nuggets of gold. We
also read every publication put out by the NTC. We eventually uncovered the principles of our playbook: the need to win the recon–counterrecon battle, the need to hit the flank, the need to mass our forces. As
Washington and Lee and Grant and Pershing and Patton and MacAr-
thur and all our great captains knew, you must be a student of military
art in order to practice it yourself."

WHOLE-TEAM PLANNING

For the junior lieutenants like myself, the climate in the 4-68 officer corps
was incredibly open, much different from what any of us expected in our
first unit. Fellow platoon leader Bobby Campbell would recall even thirty
years later, "The leadership let us have fun with it. We had a group of leaders that were very . . . *nonregimental*, if you will. They disregarded rules—
not to disregard, but because some of them didn't make sense. They were a
group of leaders who understood what the rules said but would also work
on the fringes of them. They gave us left and right boundaries that were
moved way outside of what most platoon leaders ever saw."

David Styles, another former captain in the operations team,
recalled how Dibella encouraged the team. This creative officer talked
with some pride at having come up with original ideas but also with
great engagement about how the team environment refined and maximized the ideas through discussions, After-Action Reviews, and trial
and error. One significant part of the wide-sector defensive play from
the playbook regarding our defensive scheme came to mind for him.

"We were going to make the enemy go where we wanted to engage
them, and everybody was brought into the decision. One idea that was
started by me was developed with the input of everybody. And no idea

was pooh-poohed. 'Ah, we can't do that.' No, it was developed; it was encouraged. And then, if it didn't work, we'd just try something else. Everybody was encouraged to participate."

Tom Piskel, the S3 (operations) officer, described Task Force 4-68 as an incredible command environment that created a unique synergy throughout the organization.

"A lust for new ideas permeated throughout the leadership," he said. "People would come back from every exercise and simulated battle with ideas. This continued throughout the actual NTC rotation as well."

Developing the playbook intensified our creative energies. We collected all the best thoughts we had at the time and codified them in an ever-improving document. The plays constantly evolved in our lead-up to NTC and even during the rotation itself. It was designed around our strengths and weaknesses as companies, platoons, and squads. The underlying concept of establishing simple, widely understood guidelines to execute complex tasks spread through many elements of the task-force operations beyond combat execution. Logistics, intelligence, and personnel applied similar principles in reshaping how they conducted combat-support functions. Maintenance and recovery leaders established simple repeatable methods for their support functions. These were, essentially, their own individualized playbooks.

THE BEST IDEAS WIN

The OPD meetings illustrate the personal nature of Dibella's involvement with the creative process. He was in the middle of it all, soliciting ideas, bringing key people together, inciting discussion, contributing his own ideas, and getting excited about new ideas every day. Within the confines of the military system of rank and seniority, Dibella was able to create a highly experimental, imaginative, results-focused environment. We dissected everything we could get our hands on about the NTC, objectively looking for evidence of what worked and what did not. Dibella was a unit commander with sixteen years of Army experience, yet he constantly and enthusiastically solicited and listened to ideas from lieutenants with only months on the job. It did not matter where or whom it came from; the best idea won.

The open and highly collaborative atmosphere broke down many ego barriers and allowed people to share their creative thoughts. In his own words, as Dibella described it thirty years later, "The idea was that we would encourage almost stream-of-consciousness in order to get that one good idea out of ten. We can't step on the bad ideas. We can't make fun of them. We can't disparage them. We have to just basically brainstorm. Nobody takes offense to the fact that I just gave you three really weird thoughts that are worthless, because maybe the next one is going to be really good. You never know that if you don't have the security to express it. We are all going to make mistakes—me probably more than anyone, because I take a lot of chances and do a lot of things that are not conformist, and I will get hammered for that occasionally. But all of you will do the same, all of you will make mistakes, and you will be forgiven for them."

He also emphasized the importance of our collaborative process, using all the tools available to a battalion commander. Dibella knew that his ratings on the OERs of his direct reports were absolutely critical to their careers as officers in the US Army. Capitalizing on this importance, he used the grading as an instrument to spread innovation. As I mentioned in part 1, he ensured it was absolutely clear that obtaining the highly valued A grade on your OER was contingent on discovering great ways of conducting operations that would improve combat effectiveness. However, discovery was not enough for an A+. The highest grade was reserved for the discovery and then effective sharing of the new idea to another outfit. The effect was to create a brotherhood of ingenuity that effectively diffused ideas throughout the organization. It was magical.

20

CREATIVITY UNLEASHED BY RESOURCE AVAILABILITY IN 4-68

The resources that Fred Dibella could reasonably apply to innovation within Task Force 4-68 were quite different from those available to a free-market enterprise or even those for a military unit over the longer term. For example, the task force already had assigned equipment according to its TO&E, so no opportunity to change or advance our weaponry was available. About 60 percent of active-duty US Army units at the time were modernized with state-of-the-art major weapon systems, but TF 4-68 fought with the equipment that was on its way out. The technologically advanced M1 Abrams tank and M2 Bradley armored fighting vehicle brought significant improvements in maneuverability and firepower, but these were not advantages we enjoyed. Nevertheless, no unit equipped with M1 and M2 has yet equaled our 9–0 performance. TF 4-68 got it done with old equipment: the M60A3 tank, originally launched nearly thirty years before our rotation, and the Vietnam-era M113 armored personnel carrier. Once again, 4-68's experience serves as a fascinating case study and a testament to the importance of leadership, training, and the proficiency of individual soldiers.

The efficient use of other critical resources—the most important being time—helped unleash the team's creativity and allowed us to optimize our tactics and strategy around the equipment we had. Devising new methods; experimenting with ideas for the playbook; trying out new techniques at the company, platoon, and squad levels; and relentlessly improving our basic combat skills were all time-intensive activities.

THE ONE-THIRD/TWO-THIRDS RULE

Readers unfamiliar with the military may not understand that the time demands for active-duty units can be overwhelming. There are hundreds of competing priorities and distractions. We have already covered how the clarity of purpose served to separate the wheat from the chaff for the task force. It gave everyone a clear understanding that our priority was combat proficiency. The time needed for creative activities in our ramp-up to the NTC would be a further prioritization of this focus. We placed a complementary importance on the precious few hours between receipt of a mission from higher headquarters and the start of that mission. This allowed for significant ingenuity at the front line during every operation. This two-pronged approach in managing time was a huge difference maker.

Dibella termed it *the one-third/two-thirds rule*. It applied to field training and to the planning of combat operations between receipt of mission and the mission's start.

As Dibella put it, "Discipline yourself and everyone so that two-thirds of the time, as a rule, has to go to the trigger pullers, to do whatever they need to do. Nobody knows that except them. It happens because you've ingrained it into yourselves and into your staff."

This simple rule was a crucial enabler of our ability to devise, test, and accept or reject new ideas.

In training exercises leading up to NTC, Dibella held to the rule and consistently left two-thirds of the time to the level below the task force. In a nine-day training exercise, we would spend three days conducting simulated engagements at the task-force level. The other six days were for the company commanders, allowing them to focus on what they felt their unit most needed. The company commanders would follow a similar process, dividing time between company-level exercises and platoon-level training. Individual tank crews received a similar treatment in their platoons. This time allowed us to develop and experiment with our new ideas.

The point was that at every level leaders could gain the precious resource of field time to work on their unit's specific strengths and weaknesses. The playbook helped to define those specific activities the unit needed to excel in, and the one-third/two-thirds rule gave them the time to actually excel. If the unit was good but not great at some activity that was critical to their role in a play, they would drill and drill until they could execute with excellence. The focus facilitated a deliberate practice of those things that were central to each unit's combat proficiency. While they were doing this, the general atmosphere allowed new ideas to percolate. The champions for an idea would have the time to try it out, to experiment, and to verify or reject the idea.

As you may recall, the playbook counted on Alpha to be "the central killing power of the task force," as Dibella described it. He also used to exclaim to every tank crew in the task force, "Nothing else matters if you don't bore-sight the gun tube!"

That process of aligning the main gun with the optical sights of the tank was absolutely crucial. If the gun and the sights were misaligned, the tank was little more than a sixty-ton moving target; it would not be able to hit targets accurately and inflict damage on the enemy.

In Alpha, we were fanatical about hitting targets; our accuracy in long-range tank gunnery was vital. Our strong complement of master gunnery school graduates constantly experimented with methods to improve our bore-sighting techniques. In MILES gunnery, you did not have to contend with range-finding systems, since the laser shot in a direct line of sight; but any slight misalignment meant that long-range shots—anything more than 2,000 meters—would miss the target.

Alpha's crews worked and worked until they devised the best techniques for aligning the sights. Then we drilled it until every crew could make a near-perfect bore sight that would stay consistent for the entire day's maneuvers every time. Without the field time and freedom to experiment, this never would have happened.

Each company and each platoon used their time to experiment and to deliberately practice their main roles in the plays time and time again. This atmosphere of experimentation engaged the creative process. Leaders developed customized training approaches. Team Bravo, who was the lead in our attack plays, needed to be great at land navigation. Bobby Campbell (former platoon leader in Bravo) spoke of a technique Bravo's commander used to hone their land-navigation skills.

"We used to have company training missions downrange Fort Carson," Campbell said, "and we'd have stand to, and Joe Moore would announce a grid, and everybody had to move to that grid for breakfast. The first unit there got to eat first. The last unit there had to serve. So we grew up with extremely high expectations."

Company commanders, platoon leaders, NCOs, and soldiers knew that Dibella and the chain of command would allow them to do what they thought best. Crews and NCOs also knew they could use prized field time to try out their most interesting ideas. It helped to bring out an outpouring of ingenuity that became a significant force multiplier.

The one-third/two-thirds rule gave everyone the time to work on the things they needed to improve. I distinctly remember the impact in my first weeks as a platoon leader. The challenges in garrison (i.e., on the post, not on maneuvers) were simple to master, but it was out in the field, during the simulated battles, where the rule made the most impact. The first simulated battle with the platoon stretched me to my limits. We ended up performing satisfactorily, but I felt absolutely clueless throughout much of the two-hour exercise.

We advanced through lightly forested rolling hills on a single enemy tank defensive position. One part of the platoon stood in overwatch while the other rolled forward to the next terrain feature. If the enemy showed themselves, the plan was that the overwatch section would fire and destroy them—quite simple in concept, and although the necessary skills would become second nature over the next twelve months, for now, I was sorely lacking. Simple tasks such as keeping track of the other tanks, our location on the map, or the placement of the enemy once we were fired on were supremely challenging. Essentially, I was a quarterback with no concept of the routes my receivers were running and an amateur's conception of what was happening in the game. I simply needed time at this early stage to be able to practice basic maneuvers with the platoon. In 4-68, I was granted that time.

CREATIVITY AND THE *SILVER LIONS PLAYBOOK*

Another powerful combat multiplier was the remarkable ingenuity that went into planning and preparing for each mission. You might wonder whether the playbook had taken creativity out of that part of the equation, but that was not the case at all. The playbook, in concert with the one-third/two-thirds rule, unleashed boundless creativity. What it did was take a significant portion of the ideation time that most units were consuming within the task-force headquarters and move that time down to the war fighters, down to the troops who would actually fight the battles. The plays greatly simplified the creation and dissemination of our task-force-level operations order, and it gave precious time to frontline leaders and soldiers, providing every soldier with the chance to brainstorm and rehearse the upcoming mission with the soldiers they

would be fighting alongside. This process unleashed tremendous ingenuity at the company and platoon levels, which, for those doing the
fighting, was clearly evident during the execution of every mission.

Dibella's experience at the Army's Command and General Staff College (CGSC) was formative for him. CGSC is an intensive graduate-level
program, whose curriculum includes leadership philosophy, military history, and the military planning and decision-making processes. Although
he appreciated the intent and professional excellence of the faculty and
enjoyed the immersive education, he was astonished at what he sensed
was the impracticality of actually using many of the methods CGSC was
teaching in the chaos of battle. His intuition led to a personal conclusion
that some of the critical processes taught at CGSC were fatally flawed.
When he moved into command, he believed that success would come if
he allowed and encouraged challenges of conventional doctrine. He set a
personal example by highlighting the impracticality of using the highly
touted nine-step planning process in developing a task-force-level operations order. He would exclaim, "You just don't have the time!"

Discussing the one-third/two-thirds rule, Dibella would later relate,
"It goes back to Command and General Staff College and the nine-
step planning process. It goes back to the idea that if you have gone
through this nine-step process and you have nine hours until you cross
the LD and you consume eight and a half of it trying to come up with
this brilliant plan with all these spectacular cross-attachments, you will
die. You'll give this plan to your team commanders, and they'll have
half an hour to try to get it out to their troops. You have to consume as
small an amount of time at the nonfighting level as possible in order to
preserve the maximum amount of time for the guys who are pulling the
triggers. They need their rest, they need to redistribute their ammunition, they need to change their socks, they need to pull maintenance on
their tank, they need to eat a decent meal, and they need to receive their
mission and do all the preparations necessary. If you don't give them
time to do all those things, they will not win the battle for you."

In my first NTC rotation, the 1-17 battalion staff would spend hours opining over the proper course of action for the upcoming battle. They religiously followed CGSC's nine-step process. It was thorough and comprehensive. Their plans included some great concepts that, as we discussed, actually helped form several cornerstones of the *Silver Lions Playbook*. However, that battalion-level activity consumed the time that the lower-level leaders needed to disseminate the orders and plans to their troops.

In several battles for 1-17, I received the operations order for the upcoming battle literally minutes before it was to begin. There was little time to get my platoon together for a rehearsal or even a clear explanation of the plan. There was no time to discuss the nuances of the terrain, the potential obstacles, the possible decision points we might encounter. No time to brainstorm what the enemy might do in response to our actions as the battle unfolded. No time to consider our possible contingencies to counter the enemy reaction. No time to engage the minds of the fellow soldiers who would do the actual fighting.

The one-third/two-thirds rule and the streamlined approach of the playbook made the experience with TF 4-68 dramatically different. We had the time to do all those things that I did not have in the 1-17 rotation, and we used it. We received the orders at lightning speed. Capitalizing on the vital resource of time, we then unleashed incredible creativity at the company, platoon, and tank crew levels. When Captain Dave Carruthers came back from an OP order briefing with Dibella, he immediately got the platoon leaders, company executive officer, and company first sergeant together to discuss the upcoming mission. Carruthers would lay out the overview of the task-force-level operation. It was always according to one of the six plays, so this was a simple task. We would then start to look at the nuances of Alpha's role and how we might best execute.

Everyone was involved in the process. We would pour over the terrain maps, looking for what might be our best spots for overwatch during the offensive operations, the best spots for defensive positions in the defensive plays, and where we might encounter the enemy in a movement to contact. We would discuss the challenges faced by the other companies and how that could affect us. Carruthers had a warrior's innate sense for how a battle might unfold, and we addressed each potential outcome.

We came up with some of our most creative approaches to executing the plays during those briefings. After copying the graphics onto our terrain maps and rehearsing the operation either in the sand or by walking through on open ground, we would go back to our platoons and repeat a similar process. The resulting engagement of every soldier knowing their place in the upcoming battle, understanding the importance of their unit's mission, and having participated in developing the actual plan for executing their part of the operation was magical.

The Hollywood vision of a small-unit leader getting orders, saddling up the troops, and ordering them into battle was not how we did things in TF 4-68. We engaged the creative spirit of every soldier. Application of the one-third/two-thirds rule to the order-generation process pushed the planning and preparation time down to the individual soldier. The tank drivers and gunners, the infantry men, the scouts, the maintenance teams, the artillery batteries, the Air Force liaison, the supporting attack helicopter pilots, the air-defense artillery platoon, the smoke-generator jeep driver—everyone had time to think through their roles in the upcoming operation. They had the time to consider contingencies, to study the terrain maps, and to devise creative methods that could be used while executing their mission. It was amazing to see how many great ideas this group of American soldiers came up with when given the time.

21

CREATIVITY UNLEASHED BY CONTINUOUS IMPROVEMENT IN 4-68

Another driving element of the atmosphere Dibella created in TF 4-68 was a constant desire to get better at any and every activity that would contribute to our combat proficiency. This ethos further unleashed creativity in every nook and cranny. Good was simply not good enough; in critical areas that would directly affect battle results, we strove for great. For our combat, combat support, and combat service support systems, this relentless quest for excellence drove several of our most important innovations. Although some of these may sound simple, the combined effect was a significant combat multiplier.

For example, to meet the requirements of the one-third/two-thirds rule, the Task Force S3 shop (operations) poured tremendous energy into improving their processes. The S3 team physically wrote and disseminated the operations order prior to each battle. Tom Piskel, the senior S3 officer, later recalled Dibella's direction to the team:

"We were working on reducing the time to get the OP order out when he challenged us. 'Tommy, you got two hours. It needs to be written, copies distributed, and rehearsed so the commanders are back to their units in two hours.' At first, it seemed impossible."

Other units were taking six to twelve hours to complete that task.

Two hours was a daunting challenge, given the technology available at the time. When the Observer–Controllers (OCs) at NTC first heard of the two-hour goal, they thought such speed of order generation was absolutely impossible. The playbook offered a head start, in that it reduced the time the battalion staff would spend devising the concept of the operation part of the OP order; but this was nowhere near enough. Piskel's operations team, the company commanders, and others worked diligently to optimize further. They devised time-saving methodologies to maximize the efficiency of deliberations in all aspects of devising the OP order. The hard-fought stability of the task force team, including not just the company commanders but also leaders from the various cross-attached units, greatly contributed to the optimization process. Piskel's staff also relentlessly pursued multiple methods to reduce the time consumed by administration in developing orders.

As he would later recount, "Things that could improve our effectiveness were tried and, if successful, incorporated as a matter of operating procedure. Then it was constant, continuous, relentless improvement."

That team improved their process every day leading up to the NTC. For example, one of the time-consuming tasks was copying graphics. Company commanders and other battalion leaders needed to leave the operations order briefing with graphic map overlays for the next day's operation. There was little technology to facilitate this at the time. The S3 officers and enlisted personnel would redraw them by hand. It was important to copy the graphics quickly and accurately.

One of the key officers in the shop would later recall, "We would bring guys in and say, 'Okay, we're going to copy graphics.' How could we do it with minimal errors? We would practice and practice. Somebody would make an overlay. Then we would bring a bunch of people in and have them copy it, see what the errors were, and then figure out the best way to copy an overlay without making errors—moving from left to right, top to bottom? We developed techniques based on whatever came out the best. It motivated us to work every day on trying to improve. We didn't have to go for approval; we developed it and then displayed proficiency."

OPTIMIZATION AND CLARITY

Another task in writing the OP order was naming the various phase lines, objectives, and other terrain features. Although this may seem trivial, to get the order written at the required speed when some key officers were operating on less than five hours of sleep for day after day, they did not want to have to spend time thinking about what names to use. They devised another improvement to the process.

One officer later recalled, "I had a little book where we wrote all those down so we would not have to waste time thinking what we were going to name phase lines or other things. One was football teams, one was fruits, one was vegetables, one was states, one was Civil War generals."

Little improvements such as this were happening throughout the task force, day after day.

The simple physical constraints of receiving an order from higher headquarters, moving the TOC (Tactical Operations Center) to the required location, and getting it set up for the commanders to have a place to review the task-force order and for the S3 team to have a place to construct the order presented many opportunities for continuous improvement. The TOC team honed the process through repetitive drills.

Dibella recalled the TOC soldiers' efforts: "They had to stop the track (M577) on order and then put out the tents and radios and maps and equipment in precisely ten minutes—no more. Typically, it takes an hour. To do that was a play from the playbook for the TOC soldiers.

Every man had a specific set of duties to execute in order to get it all done. They all did it exactly the same way every time. Then, when they mastered that, we would take out one man (simulating a casualty) and create an alternate play with one less player."

They would set up the entire TOC to best facilitate the issuance of tactical orders, especially at night or in adverse weather. "I wanted all the leaders warm and dry when we put out orders. Then you get their full attention."

One of the operations team captains told a memorable story of an improvement that actually happened after the first battle at NTC. He was the officer who manned the command M113 that Dibella used during operations.

"This was the very first battle that we'd fought at NTC," he said. "As we were getting near the end of the fight, we finally had units going onto the objective, and we had put some names of some objectives in our graphic piece of the order that were somewhat confusing, and nobody had caught it. As we went through planning, briefing, and rehearsal, we really did not catch the fact that these names sounded so much alike that when you are in the heat of battle, transmitting by radio, they just led to confusion.

"So here we are, the battle is in this incredibly critical stage—getting onto the objective. Fred is trying to direct units, and of course, it's Murphy's Law. That weakness in the plan, as small as it was, is starting to manifest itself, and people aren't really understanding where Fred wants them to go. And he became incredibly frustrated.

"I remember he had an alcohol marker, and he threw it at my chest and he goes, 'All this work! We're right here, and I can't get units where I need them to go because our graphics aren't right.'"

The officer's reaction was, "Crap, I can't believe I did that."

They both look back on this incident with humor now, but the names on the graphics were never unclear again.

After months of honing the process, Piskel's operations team, in collaboration with the task force's leaders, were able to get the time needed for order generation and dissemination down to Dibella's desired goal. It was fast and furious, but it was not rushed. The collaborative process that had been such a hallmark in developing the playbook was still alive and well in the work that led to the generation of the individual OP orders. The commanders and other task-force leaders had input, and plans evolved and changed prior to their completion, just as they might if hours and hours had been consumed in the nine-step process. What the framework of the playbook and personnel stability provided was an opportunity for communication to be concise and highly efficient.

It also provided time for a quick rehearsal with the commanders. Again, a dedication to continuous improvement facilitated the process. Captain Dave Styles would construct a thirty or forty-foot sand table outside the TOC for every operations order. The sand table was essentially a three-dimensional representation of the terrain over which the ensuing operation would take place. After much practice, he perfected a technique for completing the large, fairly detailed sand table in about ten minutes. Dibella and the commanders would walk through the operation with their bodies representing the location of their units.

As Dibella explained the exercise, "Even though it was essentially a play from the playbook and even though we had drilled it over and over, I wanted it rehearsed on foot in the sand table, with each member of the combat and combat-support elements walking through their part. The most beneficial part of that rehearsal is that we could war-game various eventualities. No plan ever goes as planned, so we war-gamed *what-ifs*. What if you get hit on the left flank here, Joe? What if you find your overwatch position mined, Dave?"

All of this served to ensure that the communication of the order—which play was called—was as clear as possible to every commander whose unit would be executing it.

The quest to constantly improve our communication was one to which we devoted considerable attention. In our 2015 interview, Dibella would note, "I don't know if there is any more important a thing than how you communicate."

SIMPLICITY OVER DOCTRINE

A simple but absolutely instrumental innovation within Task Force 4-68 was with our soldier-to-soldier radio communication techniques. At the time, the Army Signal Corps had developed a comprehensive set of radio and telephone procedures that were taught in basic training and used throughout the Army. By following the protocols, enemy intelligence would have difficulty extracting valuable information. The OPFOR was known to tap into insecure communication networks to gain critical intelligence or to create confusion with false reports or jammed signals. The OPFOR's reputation would seemingly make it even more important to follow the Signal Corps procedures; however, in Task Force 4-68 we were empowered to challenge such assumptions.

Our issue with the procedures was that their foundational intent was to ensure secure conversations. Task Force 4-68 decided that the foundational intent of our radio procedures should be effective communication, not security. Dibella's experience communicating as a pilot of Cobra attack helicopters contrasted significantly with the Signal Corps procedures for ground units. Aerial combat moved at fast speeds, and instant communication was essential. Pilots had no time for long call signs or formal radio procedures. Dibella brought this same sense of urgency to our combined arms task force. The slight risk of the enemy figuring out our call signs and causing confusion was worth the reward of efficient and timely communication.

Given the green light to experiment with more-effective communication techniques, we developed several that were critical to our command and control and overall success. Simplicity, brevity, and clarity were 4-68's foundations for communications. One striking example is the use of common call signs. Under the Signal Corps procedures, all of the line officers, including me, would receive a small book that contained the radio security information that friendly units would use for the next week or until a new edition came out. This booklet included the radio frequencies on which the various units of 4-68 would communicate, as well as a coded index with the encoded identifiers or call signs of each individual unit and radio operator. Each day these call signs would change. On several occasions in field operations outside of 4-68, the inability to immediately recall a fellow tank's call sign or other such minutia caused me to waste vital seconds looking it up to make simple radio calls.

In Alpha Company, we developed a simple call sign scheme to enhance clarity at the nominal expense of security. Green would indicate a headquarters unit. Red would be first platoon (my platoon); yellow, second platoon; blue, third platoon; and a new color for any attached unit. The platoon leader would be designated *one*, the platoon sergeant's tank was *two*, and so on. My call sign was *Red One*. The platoon's fourth tank was *Red Four*. It was simple, clear, and brief—as well as easy to remember.

As an example, consider the following two conversations exchanging the same critical information. Under the radio and telephone procedures, it would go like this:

> "Whiskey Alpha Juliet One Seven, this is Whisky Alpha Juliet Two Six. What is happening to your front? Over."

> "Whisky Alpha Juliet Two Six, this is Whiskey Alpha Juliet One Seven. Negative activity to front. Over."

> "Whiskey Alpha Juliet One Seven, this is Whisky Alpha Juliet Two Six. Roger out."

With the simplified call signs, this conversation would be greatly shortened. You would not need to have memorized your call sign for the day or that of your fellow tank commander. The conversation would go more like this:

> "Red Two, this is Red One. What is happening to your front? Over."

> "Red One, this is Red Two. Negative activity to front. Over."

> "Red Two, this is Red One. Roger out."

Another innovation was the use of a company-wide net, again counter to accepted procedures. Doctrine at the time would have the company headquarters and platoon leaders on one net (radio frequency) and the platoon on a separate net. Platoon leaders had a radio that could switch between the nets, depending on to whom they needed to talk. The intent was to ensure that no single net was overloaded with traffic.

Again, we found this approach to be less than optimal. Simplifying the call signs eliminated much of the unneeded traffic, and the clarity brought about when all fourteen tank commanders in the company heard the same thing was transformational. Soon all of the 4-68 maneuver companies were operating on a single company net. I can't say enough about how much this helped improve command and control.

It was also an excellent training aid. After the Armor Basic Officer Leaders Course, which had drilled in the Signal Corps communication methodologies, the conversion to common call signs was liberating; but I still did not feel my communications were as crisp as they could be. This changed in a week because of the common company command net.

A fellow platoon leader was unable to deploy for a short field exercise. As a result, Sergeant First Class Roacha, his platoon sergeant, served as the acting platoon leader for third platoon. In that one week on the company-wide radio net, I was able to listen and learn from this experienced NCO as he conducted incredibly effective, clear, concise, simple communications with a tank platoon. The experience was invaluable. By emulating many of the techniques SFC Roacha used, my ability to effectively communicate during combat operations immeasurably improved. Without the company-wide net, this never would have happened.

Following that experience, the earlier conversation would be even simpler:

"Red 2? Red 1. Sit-rep?"

"This is 2. All quiet. Over."

"Roger out."

CLEAR AND CONCISE

There were several other notable advancements in our communications that illustrate the constant drive to improve. Brevity and clarity in what was said on the radio and written in operations orders was tantamount. To that end, Dibella and key members of the operations staff undertook exercises to help them hone their skills.

One of these was a drill he invented: Two people would stand back to back. One would face a white board with a dry erase marker in hand, and the other would have a geometric design on paper similar to the one below.

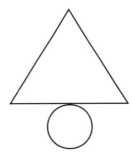

The task would be for the person with the design to describe it as concisely and as specifically as possible to the person at the white board, never seeing the resulting effort. The person at the board would attempt to draw what was being described. A key part of the exercise was that the white board artist was not permitted to speak. It was a totally one-way transmission, like transmitting in the blind over a radio. When the transmitter was finished, he turned around to see what had been drawn. With the initial attempts, it was usually humorous, but the exercise was illuminating. As they worked and worked at it, it was eventually near perfect.

Although it may sound like a basic exercise, those who participated learned valuable lessons about the communication process: what was said, what was heard, how unintended things can be communicated, how precision matters, how the beginning of a conversation sets the framework for the entire conversation, how people can have different definitions for the same term, how important it can be to establish a consistent use of common words to describe things, and more. All of this would trickle down into the OP order generation process, the communications over the command radio net, and even face-to-face everyday interactions. Try this with some friends or coworkers, and you'll immediately understand its value.

The ultimate objective of the exercise was for the officers involved to be able to deliver communications over the radio so emphatically, so specifically, and so confidently that there was little to no chance of misunderstanding. This kind of one-way transmission was often necessary when bullets were flying in the heat of battle. That is when it has to be short, unambiguous, and compelling, because a simple misunderstanding could be deadly.

The focus on effective communication over the task-force command radio net greatly contributed to the winning result. On this secure network, 4-68 most blatantly violated the Signal Corps protocols.

Dibella recalled, "We got dinged on it terribly by the comms controllers."

To add some levity to the harsh evaluations, he would play snippets of key communications from the just-finished battle in the After-Action Reviews, emphasizing the clarity of the information exchange and the impact such exchanges had on actions. He would poke fun at the violations of protocol. He also labored to ensure that the command net was a source of coordination and collaboration among the company commanders.

One officer recalled, "Fred was not a commander who dominated the command net during a battle. He would always encourage the commanders to talk to each other. If that wasn't happening to a sufficient degree, he would put out a net call for them to start doing it, because we were at our best when those commanders were talking to each other."

The philosophy of driving authority and accountability to the front line resonated in our communication techniques and in the count-less improvements made to the manner and specificity of individual communications. 4-68 would not suffer the type of defeat that 1-17 experienced in their brigade-coordinated attack. In that battle, a mis-communication on the brigade command net resulted in the main ele-ments of a task force marching right into the same OPFOR kill zone in which their sister task force had just been annihilated. Unequivocal exchange of critical information, given all the confusion created by the dense fog of war, drove the communication improvements in 4-68 and contributed significantly to the positive end result.

These kinds of simple, small innovations were happening all over the task force. Activities became more streamlined, communications more clear, maintenance actions quicker and more robust, chemical warfare decontamination more swift, artillery support more accurate and deadly, air support more precise and timely, resupply more timely, and count-less other actions more focused. Instead of death by a thousand cuts, as happened with many units at NTC, it was exceptional execution by a thousand simple improvements to conventional methods.

A LASTING EFFECT

Similar to the study of leadership themes at Gallup, military historians study the great commanders of the past in seeking to define the character attributes that account for their successes. In Alexander the Great we see unbounded ambition; Julius Caesar, inspirational charisma; George Washington, dogged composure; Erwin Rommel, extreme cunning; George S. Patton, unabashed audacity. If they go to war, these command-ers leave an indelible mark on history. Those that prepare for war but do not see the bloody carnage of that most primal of human devastations also leave a mark. It is most noticeable in those that they have led.

These military leaders are magicians in a sense, blending their unique individual talents with an extraordinary ability to inspire heroic actions in what are often the most demanding situations. Like death-defying magic acts, their armies or units accomplish what seems impossible. If we look deep enough, we find a common thread: These commanders unleash incredible ingenuity within the nucleus of their armies, a creativity that amplifies those armies' lethality in the crucible of battle and brings forth victory in what objectively appear to be no-win situations. Alexander would not have conquered the known world against enemies that outnumbered his army over five to one without the honed perfection of his legendary phalanx or the ingenious shock and awe of Macedonia's Companion Cavalry.

Fred Dibella did not have the opportunity to command a great army in actual battle, but he did lead a task force of some 600 soldiers to achieve something unique. In the process, the collective ingenuity of that group of men resulted in the advancement of several new conceptual approaches and innovative methods for fighting modern maneuver warfare. We all hope that in some way it has made a lasting contribution.

Back in 1986, the stories of an M60A3 battalion that had beaten the invincible OPFOR spread throughout the Army like wildfire. A great deal of what we developed was absorbed into the psyche of the Officer Corps and surfaced in many different forms during the maneuver battles of both Gulf Wars, unquestionably creating our most valued legacy—saving American lives. To anyone reading whose execution in those wars gained some small assistance by these concepts, I can speak for Fred Dibella, his higher-level leaders, and all the soldiers of the Silver Lions: We are supremely humbled. We could not be more thankful that the ideas developed in this extraordinary command environment had a lasting impact. To those whom these concepts may assist in the future, Godspeed.

22

PURPOSE-DRIVEN

CREATIVITY AT STRYKER

Spanning three decades and involving thousands of employees, Stryker's innovations made lasting contributions in the medical-device field and the healthcare industry. Propelled by the creative crucibles of its development labs and an idea-focused approach to acquisitions, a good portion of Stryker's ingenuity was expressed in the form of new products and services. Complementing these efforts, the burning need to achieve consistent growth over time sparked ingenuity throughout the company. Similar to the breadth of creative ideas within Task Force 4-68, Stryker's endless quest for 20-percent earnings growth inspired innovation across the broad spectrum of enterprise activities.

In fact, other medical-device companies were devoting larger percentages of their total revenues toward research and development efforts. Stryker kept R&D expenses to about 5–7 percent of revenues. Medtronic, another fast-growing medical-device manufacturer at the time, was spending upward of 10 percent. Most of our other competitors were also outspending Stryker on a relative basis. The story of

Stryker's ingenuity includes highly efficient use of its R&D dollar and the determined application of creative energies beyond the products envisioned and developed in the R&D lab or acquired by the company. Building a better mousetrap did not mean the world would beat a path to our door. The approach was to build the better mousetrap and construct a highly traveled, multilane superhighway between our customer's door and our door.

A significant advancement in product features or the introduction of new product categories might generate growth for a few quarters or even years for some divisions, but 20 percent every quarter, every year, required constant stimulus. Innovation had to happen in sales and marketing, in corporate structure and approach, in recruiting, in operations, in human resources, in internal systems and processes, and in leadership. The 20-percent goal created a tension that unleashed creative juices in all these areas.

Growth drivers reviewed every year during strategic-planning exercises included not just new products or acquisitions but also new systems, new manufacturing processes, new marketing programs, new sales techniques, new talent, new IT systems, new management tools, and many other initiatives targeted to create the opportunities for earnings growth. Nurturing these many drivers was top of mind for every senior manager and divisional leader. The simple *invent it, make it, sell it* mantra called for creative energies in all areas.

Looking back during our 2015 conversation, John Brown emphasized the impact of Stryker's purpose on the widespread quest for innovation:

"It was all about the goal setting," he said. "The goal was so firmly entrenched in everybody's mind on a day-to-day basis that it forced everyone to think about innovative products, but not just innovation in products—innovative ways to do things. It forced everybody to focus on trying to do their job better. As a result, the company was always looking ahead employee by employee."

The conditions fostered and the 20-percent goal urged ingenuity throughout the business. The goal of 20-percent growth gave a clear purpose to innovation. When combined with significant resource availability and a pervasive philosophy of continuous improvement, Stryker's atmosphere served to unleash phenomenal creativity within and throughout the organization.

ENCOURAGING OUT-OF-THE-BOX THINKING

Dr. Homer Stryker started his company partly as an outlet for his own ingenuity. Unlike the oppressive situation Dibella inherited at 4-68 Armor, Brown walked into an environment with a tinkerer's passion for refining and experimenting. However, the prevailing sentiments toward innovation were on a small scale. To grow at 20 percent per year, the reserved Stryker team would require a phase shift. Stryker would need to get ahead of impending technological advancements in the medical-device field and demonstrate a capacity to scale its sales, marketing, and manufacturing efforts. It was a huge challenge to stimulate broader thinking and a view beyond the current product offerings.

To accomplish this, Brown set an example by personally spearheading one of the company's first acquisitions. When its maverick new CEO proposed acquiring an orthopedic implant company with plans to grow its New Jersey–based business, such an action was way out of the box. This action had far-reaching effects on the creative psyche of the company's employees, similar to the introduction of the playbook concept to Task Force 4-68. Just as challenging Army doctrine with the idea of operational plays served to unshackle the creative juices within TF 4-68, the acquisition of Osteonics by Stryker's energetic young CEO served to shatter preconceived notions about what the company would do to grow. It began a profound release of creative energies and a broadening of perspectives within the close-knit boutique device firm out of Kalamazoo.

"When we acquired Osteonics—" Brown said in our 2015 conversation, "—this is right after we'd gone public, '79. I had been with the company about two and a half years. Osteonics had a unique and new hip [replacement] design. Two engineers founded the company. They had another engineer that worked for them and a secretary/administrative assistant—so, four people. I spent a good bit of time with them. I went to New Jersey several times, and we were literally sitting on mail cages because of how short of funds they were. Finally we agreed on a deal, and I presented it to Stryker's directors and brought the two principals out. We had them spend an afternoon with the board. At the end of the meeting, the board said, quote, 'These guys are crazy. You should have no business trying to do a deal with them.'"

For the young John Brown, it was the ideas and the technology that mattered. The fact that these engineers did not appear to be seasoned business managers was unimportant. They had superb, patentable concepts and a design that showed great promise.

Brown further explained his conversation with the board as he defended his position: "They were eccentric, but they were smart. And so I said, 'Well, I've already given them a $50,000 down payment.' The board really was somewhat annoyed. So finally they said to me, 'All right, we will approve this deal for the company. But you better make sure it works, because if it doesn't, you're out of here.' It was probably one of the best deals we ever did."

He did not attempt to grow Stryker's sales by purchasing existing revenue streams from a large, existing firm. Instead, he went after a small company with a creative group of people who had good ideas that could be nurtured and grown over time. Osteonics would grow briskly and later become the largest and most profitable operating division of the company. The acquisition revitalized the creative process. Stryker's new CEO went out on a limb, against the conservative advice of the board of directors, and purchased a company that had little more than a novel product design in a related—but different—market. This marked a turning point in Stryker's process of unleashing creativity.

A later annual report looked back on the situation in 1977, when Brown arrived: "Product lines had become static, and only the manufacture of bone screws represented any real attention to the important orthopedic implant market."

By broadening the outlook beyond the labs of the company's quaint little building in Kalamazoo, Brown ignited a transformation that would see incredible ingenuity spring forth from all areas.

ENERGIZING CREATIVITY

This same report noted, "The revitalization that began with the recruitment of Brown was all-encompassing. A five-year plan was launched that called for the development of new product lines, new business strategies, new management techniques, and a leadership approach that managed assets."

As Brown worked to unleash creativity in all these areas, new products, further acquisitions of early-stage companies with inventive ideas, and a revitalization of the company's leadership served to drive the growth of the company for those first five years. Actions such as the acquisition of Osteonics were part of an evolutionary process that would continue in successive five-year periods as the company embraced the 20-percent growth goal and continued expansion. Each step of the way pivotal decisions would further stoke the creative fires.

Such broadening of the scale for creative ideas was an important factor in the decision to divide the company into focused divisions. Brown described the management environment when he first joined: "Lee [Stryker, the company's president before Brown], bless his heart, had about fifteen people reporting to him, so it was a very flat organization. Lee was making all the major decisions personally."

It was not a leadership technique conducive to unleashing creativity on a broad scale. As a result, Brown made changes.

"I restructured that approach and started delegating authority, which was somewhat new to Stryker."

This restructuring gained benefits, but it was still not yet unleashing the level of creativity Brown believed was needed to sustain 20-percent growth.

"I must admit that in the first three or four years, every major decision still had to come across my desk." He took further action. "I finally realized that I was the biggest problem in the company. That's when we started really forming the divisions and delegating authority. And that paid off handsomely."

At the time, Stryker had been a company for over four decades, and many long-term employees had grown accustomed to the founder's central control. Delegating authority and accountability, restructuring the organization, and embracing new modes of thinking served to break the old patterns.

Sales structure and compensation were one of the first areas to benefit from the creative process. Exercising their newfound autonomy, sales managers and leaders completed the conversion to direct company representatives with compensation paid at 100-percent commission for the company's traditional product lines. They began the rack and stack process, ranking representatives by their individual and regional performances. Openly displaying the performance of each representative and ranking them on order volume, growth, and percentage to quota became company policy. By 1980, the team selling Stryker's traditional products split into two. Greater intimacy with a narrowed group of customers led to greater intimacy with advancing surgical and healthcare requirements, all of which fed back into the R&D and marketing teams, beginning a productive cycle of idea and information exchange among the customer, the sales representative, the marketing professional, and the engineer.

Taking further bold steps, Stryker established its first foreign subsidiary in Germany in 1979, and by 1984 the company had converted from a distributor network to a direct-sales force in Australia, West Germany, and the Netherlands. Many of the newly developed sales management, motivational, and recruitment approaches from the US office applied to the international efforts as well. But the overseas leaders were also empowered to exercise their own creativity and to do what they thought best for their particular markets and country cultures. The international sales efforts saw an explosion of creativity when the country managers were given wide authority to develop their organizations as they saw fit. This even included acquiring small manufacturing companies. The Stryker constants were ever present: 20-percent growth, empowerment, authority and accountability, and support of those closest to the customer.

PUSHING A MANUFACTURING RENAISSANCE

Courageous steps and key acquisitions punctuated Stryker's first decade as a public company. The burgeoning creative spirit worked its way through the departments, but it took considerable time to reach the stolid manufacturing plants. With constantly increasing sales and expanding product offerings, the manufacturing teams were highly stretched just keeping up with production demands. Meeting the FDA's evolving Good Manufacturing Practice requirements, implementing modernized Materials Requirements Planning (MRP II) information systems, and making the ever-increasing monthly build counts were challenging requirements. As a result, Stryker's fundamental manufacturing capabilities did not advance much in Brown's first ten to twelve years.

When I joined the company in 1989, there was still a great deal of the old sentiment lingering in the Medical division manufacturing plant. The impending transformation further unleashed creativity within the company. It also gave me the chance to experience firsthand how the environment John Brown created stoked those creative fires.

Entering Stryker Medical's manufacturing facility in 1989 as a young project manager fresh out of the military was a memorable experience. One of the lasting impressions was how similar the factory appeared to what I had studied of World War II–era manufacturing in America. As a student of the war, I had learned of the industrial machinery used in the great American mobilization, when US industry outproduced all of the other combatants on both sides combined. What I saw in the Stryker plant were processes and equipment similar to those used during the war. Although this may have been nostalgic, manufacturing processes had evolved considerably between 1945 and 1989, and Stryker had not entirely kept up.

The most sophisticated machine was an outdated Computer Numerically Controlled (CNC) milling center. This monstrous apparatus was used to make only one part, the bases for hydraulic jacks, which were key components for all of the hospital stretchers. The assembly of about 80 percent of the products that shipped from the facility could not start without this jack base. The machining cycle for the base had been programmed long ago, and there was a general lack of enthusiasm to attempt any improvements. It was a 1970s-era device, its instructions entered by reading a tape whose perforations could only be made by another device that was off-site at a sister division. There was no impetus to route any new parts to the machine, because suppliers had much more modern equipment that could easily beat its run times and production costs.

The other primary fabrication processes were hand welding, metal cutting, bending, and shaping with WW II–era machinery, a manual lathe, and manual machining. You might think that in such a manufacturing environment the furthest thing from the realm of possibility would be process innovation. Certainly, there would be no appetite for a complete revamp of the plant. Nonetheless, that is exactly what happened over the next five years.

When my project responsibilities began to include the production capability of the plant, the senior manufacturing engineers and floor supervisors advised that "Corporate" would never approve new machinery. They had tried and failed to receive approval for a CNC lathe, and that was that. I felt that the operations team had simply not yet grasped the new paradigm. The company had loads of cash on the balance sheet, and all we needed to do was present viable proposals that would drive bona fide earnings growth. With a new creative manufacturing engineer joining the team, the process began.

Over the next four years, we championed dozens of capital expenditure requests through the corporate office, each showing the clear payback for the new machinery to the bottom line—essentially, how it would contribute to 20-percent earnings growth. Brown and CFO Dave Simpson met personally with my team members and me several times during this process. At first they wanted to ensure that we knew what we were doing, but after several years, their interests shifted to what we were doing and how we were delivering such solid cost reductions.

Brown would comment on the manufacturing revolution happening in the Medical Division in his monthly letters. In Stryker's highly competitive environment, this served to inspire other divisions to supercharge their own manufacturing improvements. The next decade would see tremendous advancements across Stryker's manufacturing divisions.

By early 1994, we had brought Medical Division's World War II–era manufacturing plant into the 1990s. The new processes included CNC vertical and horizontal machining centers, CNC multiaxis lathes, advanced cut-off saws, Single Minute Exchange of Die (SMED) capability for our presses, state-of-the-art long-bed CNC machining centers, CNC tube bending, and fully integrated robotic welding systems. We also added on to the facility to bring powder coating on-site, greatly simplifying the flow of parts to the assembly lines.

After five years, the fabrication capability was unrecognizable compared with the outmoded plant of 1989. In the process, we worked very hard, hired a lot of new people, facilitated training for existing employees, and had a great deal of fun. The introduction of the new machinery in the plant further unleashed creative juices on the factory floor and in the development labs.

Industrial engineers, supervisors, and machine operators continually devised new and better ways of exploiting the new machinery capabilities. As understanding of our new fabrication capabilities spread, it ignited multiple initiatives in purchasing and planning to insource complicated and expensive purchased components. It also greatly increased our leverage in negotiations with suppliers, since they understood that we could do more and more in-house.

The new capabilities also spawned an explosion of creativity in component design and design for manufacturability—engaging the factory floor and manufacturing teams. R&D engineers replaced what had been time-consuming, two-day trips to key suppliers for reviewing potential designs with simple walks into the fabrication area and discussions with machine operators, industrial, or quality engineers. As a result of such collaboration, many employees on the factory floor no longer felt they were just making a widget in a repetitive process. They were a part of the design and quality of an end product.

The empowered environment that allowed such a complete revamping of a manufacturing plant proliferated throughout the company. Similar things happened at the Instruments building across town, at Endoscopy in Silicon Valley, and at Osteonics in New Jersey. The unleashing of creativity that began in sales and marketing spread to engineering and business development, then into operations, human resources, customer service, quality assurance, and all throughout the company. People were given the autonomy to go after the ideas and initiatives they felt would deliver results. Twenty-percent earnings growth stood as the guidepost. In this atmosphere, game-changing ideas that could affect the bottom line also came from people in departments far from the development labs.

GALVANIZING PRODUCT CREATION

John Brown's inaugural letter to the shareholders described the importance of product development: "Our goal is to increase sales through the development or acquisition of new products so as to maintain a level of earnings growth in excess of 20 percent a year."

Each successive annual report highlighted the new products, major product improvements, and product acquisitions that generated increased sales that year and were expected to do so in the years ahead. In the early 2000s, an outside consulting group came into Stryker to assist with a company-wide branding effort. What they quickly recognized was how crucial innovation was throughout the company. However, Stryker's brand of innovation had a distinctive twist: The company desired innovation that endured.

John Brown's influence on product innovation is particularly illuminating, because his decentralization of authority allowed the company's divisions to innovate in the best way for them, all firmly centered on producing growth. The significantly different approaches are a further testament to the extreme empowerment. Following their chosen model, each division built success with hundreds of important but relatively small breakthroughs and advancements. If there was a common theme, it was that no division participated in huge markets where a single hit, such as the world's best search algorithm (Google) or the world's most popular operating system (Microsoft), or becoming the lowest-cost provider of a vital commodity (Standard Oil), could create a financial behemoth. Stryker's divisions had to earn their growth the hard way, slugging it out with competitors in small- to medium-sized markets

NO END IN SIGHT FOR ENDOSCOPY

Stryker's surgical products started on the acquisition and engineering path very early in Brown's tenure. In 1978, the company entered the developing arthroscopy (an instrument for minimally invasive joint surgery) market, launching the Orthoscope, Stryker's first fiber-optic lens for arthroscopy. Following the template of acquiring early-stage technologies, Stryker then acquired a minority position in its primary supplier of optical equipment for those arthroscopy products, Tele-SynOptics. In the ensuing years, SynOptics continued to introduce improved scopes and cameras, including many that expanded into the burgeoning endoscopy market. By 1989, Stryker had purchased the remaining portion of Syn-Optics and spawned its own Endoscopy Division, which would incorporate most of the former SynOptics employees, including the innovative William Chang, who would become the notable vice president of R&D for Endoscopy.

Over the next decade, Stryker Endoscopy became a primary contributor to that period of growth John Brown would refer to as *the long run*. Out of the creative crucible of Chang's R&D labs in Santa Clara, the division developed and launched series after series of best-in-class surgical camera and medical video-imaging systems that increased sales and earnings. As the use of less-invasive procedures gained momentum within the medical community, Stryker Endoscopy also grew significantly faster than the market, outpacing its competitors by proliferating innovative products and solutions.

New products outside the imaging category broadened Stryker's market stance, and the launch of a soup-to-nuts integrated suite of endoscopy products took the business to the next level. Capitalizing on its success, Endoscopy would later spin off a new division focused on communications in the operating theater. Devising its own unique approach to delivering 20-percent earnings growth, with significant product advancements and innovations, Stryker Endoscopy became a top player in the minimally invasive surgery equipment market and a constant contributor to 20-percent growth.

FOCUSED ENGINEERING AND TARGETED ACQUISITIONS AT INSTRUMENTS

While all of this was happening, the Surgical Instruments Division became a hotbed for focused engineering and targeted acquisitions, all of which flourished in that division's particular version of the creative atmosphere Brown allowed to be unleashed.

Stryker's 1983 launch of a new line of battery-powered, cordless, heavy-duty orthopedic instruments gave surgeons more freedom of movement than the pneumatic instruments of the day, without sacrificing performance. Quickly realizing that battery power would be the wave of the future, the practical-minded Instruments team soon understood that the design and manufacture of small DC motors that could survive sterilization would be essential to their success.

Over two decades of relentless product and process innovation, Stryker became the world's leader in such specialized motors. The team developed an absolute passion to integrate state-of-the-art battery technology in their surgical products. They built deep supplier and consulting relationships to stay on the leading edge. Insightfully, the team also realized that becoming the highest-quality, lowest-cost manufacturer of blades for these instruments was absolutely crucial to achieving the 20-percent growth purpose. They poured incredible talent and resources into ensuring that high-quality, low-cost formula would always work to their favor.

In the 1990s, as the AIDS epidemic spread and the awareness of blood-borne pathogens expanded in the medical community, solutions to safeguard surgeons, nurses, and technicians in the operating theater saw increased demand. Seizing the opportunity, Instruments' agile business development team identified a small, early stage company called Steri-Shield, which offered a line of personal protective gear for use in surgery. Once brought into the fold in the Instruments Division, the team set to work proliferating the product line, revamping manufacturing, and growing sales. Over time, Steri-Shield became a significant contributor to growth and profitability. Successful integration and assimilation of these types of small product-line acquisitions became a mainstay of the growth strategy at Instruments and a core competence of the division.

IMPLANTING GROWTH THROUGH SCIENCE

The implant divisions developed a wide array of new products and often led the evolution of materials science as it applied to implants. Stryker

expanded its breadth of implant offerings through acquisitions championed by the international divisions, corporate headquarters, and Osteonics. As the company's presence in the implant markets grew, a clear
distinction in Stryker's approach emerged.

To meet the relentless 20-percent growth requirement, the underlying creative atmosphere centered on a scientist's focus to deliver clinical results. The company had to be discerning in determining whether
the latest advancements in surgical techniques were passing fads or the
beginnings of major new trends. Piling onto an explosive fad in one year
that faded in the next would not be a successful formula for consistent
20-percent-growth performance over time. One notable example illustrates the approach.

In the late 1990s, one of Stryker's largest competitors began pushing
a new method of performing hip-replacement surgery. This competitor had developed a set of instrumentation and implants that allowed
a minimally invasive total-hip arthroplasty. Minimally invasive techniques had revolutionized surgical procedures in a variety of special-
ties over the past decade. Laparoscopic cholecystectomy transformed
gall-bladder removals from an involved, large-incision, open procedure with lengthy recovery time to a same-day surgery in which many
patients could walk out the day of the procedure and be mostly recov-
ered within days instead of weeks. With the competitor's aggressive
marketing of such minimally invasive advantages to hip replacements,
many saw this procedure as the next wave.

Despite having expertise in hip replacements and a sister division
that was a leader in equipment for minimally invasive procedures,
Stryker did not immediately pour its resources into this new idea.
For about two years, the technical and financial press highly criticized
Stryker for being late to the game and moving too slowly in convert-
ing to what many analysts believed was the future of hip replacements.
Even though the company earnings continued to grow at 20 percent
or more, many saw this recalcitrance as a sign that Stryker was being

passed by in innovation. The company moved slowly until the instruments, technology, and technique evolved.

The ethos at Stryker was for innovation that endured. The implant division did not move guns blazing into minimally invasive hip replacement because the scientists believed it might be a fad or at least needed additional nurturing and evolution before it would become mainstream. An analysis of the available outcomes data as well as an in-depth understanding of the practical shortcomings involved with the minimally invasive process led Stryker to conclude that the technology available at the time did not deliver an enduring tangible benefit for many patients. Stryker wanted a longer look at actual recovery times from the procedure. Early data indicated that it might actually lengthen the longer-term recovery time by six or nine months.

The scientists knew that the access a surgeon gains in a traditional procedure helps them accurately align the implant onto the patient's bones. With limited access in the minimally invasive procedures, this alignment would more difficult. Proper alignment is a key element for long-term patient outcomes, and Stryker's scientists were not convinced that any but the very best and most-skilled surgeons would achieve equivalent alignment with the tools initially available for these procedures. Later studies by the American Academy of Orthopedic Surgeons, Harvard Medical Center, and others would confirm Stryker's cautious approach. Today the tools and techniques for minimally invasive hip replacements are much more evolved, but the traditional procedure is still frequently performed. Osteonics took a deliberate, methodical approach into developing and marketing its own offering, despite the constant pleas from analysts and investor groups.

This example illustrates the difference in thinking between a Stryker leader who lived in constant vigilance, knowing that 20-percent growth was an every-year phenomenon, and the leaders of other companies who might seek the immediate benefit of a one-hit wonder. It is somewhat counterintuitive that the company demanding 20-percent growth every quarter would actually be more circumspect in deciding whether they would follow a potential new trend. The distinctly creative approach toward new products and new instrumentation at Osteonics centered on long-term clinical outcomes and sound medical science.

CREATING NEW CATEGORIES IN EMS EQUIPMENT

There is perhaps no better illustration of the medical product business's unique innovative model than the history of the EMS business. Stryker EMS launched into a global market that was at best growing only 2–3 percent annually and, in some years, shrinking. As a new entrant into the market, Stryker's initial years were focused on capturing market share with a flanking attack on a monopoly competitor. After five or six years of success, gaining over 50-percent share in the United States, the chances to continue 20-percent earnings growth just fighting it out with this competitor were slim; the market would not support it. As a result, we were forced to find other ways to expand. Our expertise and strengths were in a maverick marketing approach supporting a highly creative R&D team. In John Brown's environment of unleashed creativity, divisions were empowered to soar with their strengths. For us, this meant developing custom products for international markets and launching new-to-the-world product categories.

Starting with the initial ambulance cots, we built the business on having a much more durable, reliable, and rugged product than what was available at the time. The actual brand name of the products was RUGGED, and the striking safety-yellow and black appearance set us apart from the raw aluminum equipment available from the competitors of the day. Our initial foray into the international markets used the same approach. We designed and built ultrarugged ambulance stretchers, customized to fit foreign ambulances. The deck heights, fastening systems, and loading methods were all different from those in the United States. Our international M1 roll-in cot system offered dramatic differences from the existing competitors yet still conformed to the local requirements. It was a growth driver.

The second prong was focused on solving significant problems facing EMS providers around the globe. Over the next decade, we developed three new product categories that dramatically improved patient handling in prehospital treatment. After several years in the business, my team realized that an emerging employee-injury crisis was facing our customer base. As patients were getting heavier, and the average EMTs lifting the patients were aging and included a higher number of females, on-the-job back injuries were soaring. In addition, the many safety issues that arose in the event of an ambulance crash were gaining awareness. Stryker EMS set off on a determined mission to provide technological solutions to these challenging issues. We worked closely with internationally recognized EMS services to identify the sources of injury, developed strong partnerships with ambulance manufacturers and regulatory bodies working on crash-worthiness, and dared our engineering and marketing talent to devise breakthrough answers to these difficult problems.

First we launched the category of *tracked EMS stair chairs*. These were foldable/storable wheeled chairs that had an innovative friction-based track system that users could deploy to provide considerable assistance when transporting people down the stairs. The StairPRO was a game-changing product. Smaller EMTs gained the capability to safely transport patients down the stairs, dramatically reducing the risks of back injury to themselves while also improving safety for the patient. As we developed the product, many focus groups loved demonstrations of the prototypes but thought such a product would be far too expensive. To do it right, the chair would end up being three to five times more costly than the seldom-used, simple folding chairs most ambulances carried at the time. We knew the injury-reduction benefits were real, and the costs of such injuries far exceeded the cost of a fleet of tracked chairs. As it turned out, the StairPRO chair saw the fastest market uptake rate of any new product Medical Division had ever launched, even at the high price.

Our second major breakthrough was a viable powered ambulance cot. Lifting patients from the ground to the upright position for moving the cot and then loading the cot into the ambulance was another source of heavy back strain driving high rates of injury. Stryker launched an innovative battery-powered, hydromechanical cot that allowed EMTs to lift patients with great ease with the press of a button. The product was a particularly challenging engineering feat, because it had to have the power and strength to assist lifting up to a 700-pound patient yet still be light and maneuverable and have no compromises in the time it took to load and unload from the ambulance. Several patented new technologies allowed all of these requirements to be met, and Power-PRO was another runaway success.

The final major breakthrough was, perhaps, the most demanding and complex product Stryker Medical ever developed. We found it odd that in most of the developed world, the process of loading garbage from a customer's curbside into a truck had converted from a physically intensive, back-injury prone, manual operation to one where the sanitation companies issued customers customized wheeled containers that could be rolled out to the curbside and then picked up and hydraulically dumped into the garbage truck. This conversion involved a multimillion-dollar infrastructure investment all over the globe. Yet critically ill patients were still being loaded into the backs of ambulances by skilled EMTs and paramedics using simply their own brute force. It was an operation riddled with significant injury risks for the providers and patients. Not infrequently, patients were dropped or tipped over during loading or unloading, resulting in injuries and lawsuits. The situation begged for a technology solution.

Like the PowerPRO, there could be no compromises. Load and unload times had to be equal to current methods; a complete and seamless manual backup had to work in the event of power loss; battery management had to be automatic; crash-worthiness had to be best in class; operation had to be simple; and it needed to be easily cleaned. In the process of addressing all these often competing requirements, the team invented and patented multiple new technologies for the loading and unloading method, near-field communication techniques between the stretcher and the loading system, inductive charging between the trolley and the cot (to recharge the batteries), and a host of other mechanisms. At launch, the PowerLoad system was well received, and it is still in the process of transforming the industry's infrastructure today. We look forward to the day when no patient has to be loaded by brute force.

With the international expansion and three breakthrough new-product categories, the EMS business was a significant growth engine, delivering a combined annual growth rate of over 25 percent during the years through 2012, when I retired. There was nothing more rewarding than to have seasoned paramedics come into our booth at trade shows and ask to hug the engineers, thanking them for creating technologies that allowed them to do their jobs without injuring themselves or patients.

The purpose-driven atmosphere unleashed creative energies to go after these game-changing innovations. Success continues in EMS. In 2016, Stryker acquired the world's leading manufacturer of EMS defibrillation for over $1.2 billion to complement the company's global market position in the prehospital market.

John Brown's first years ushered in an explosion of ingenuity in product creation and refinement all over the company. All of it was very purposeful.

As Brown put it, "I'd say the goal-motivated innovation—and not just a goal that was imposed on them but a goal that we all agreed on—was a good idea. We all endorsed it, loved it."

As was noted in the very first annual report, innovation was focused on those projects and acquisitions intended to drive 20-percent earnings growth. It was mostly evolutionary, not revolutionary. John Brown fashioned an environment that captured the hearts and energies of Stryker's engineers, marketing professionals, and business development people, enabling them to develop their own innovative models and create or acquire the hundreds of products needed to achieve 20-percent growth for twenty-eight years in a row.

23

RESOURCE

AVAILABILITY

AT STRYKER

Three critical resources stood above all others when it came to unleashing the creativity at Stryker: time, capital funding, and headcount. Each of them was constrained, but instead of throttling the creative process, these constraints served to bring a determined focus and a problem-solving mindset to innovators. In the attempt to achieve aggressive growth, many companies tend to overspend and overreach.

Growth for a capitalist enterprise tends to create a boom-and-bust cycle. At Stryker it would have been natural to see periods of rapid growth followed by slower times or even small declines. Part of the ethos of maintaining such consistency was a predictable approach to allocating critical resources toward new ideas and initiatives. Although there might be a tendency to apportion a few more funding or headcount resources when a division or even the entire corporation exceeded the 20-percent benchmark, considerable resources would also be applied toward growth when divisions were just making the number. In those periods, departments throughout the division would search diligently for new tools and techniques that would help reignite growth.

A SWAMP FULL OF ALLIGATORS

In almost all periods, finding the time to innovate was the first challenge. With 20-percent growth constantly adding daily demands, it was daunting just to keep up. Setting aside time to create and implement new methods or improve processes was often challenging.

A befitting allegory for Stryker employees was a "swamp full of alligators." Imagine yourself in the middle of a swamp filled with scores of alligators. It is pouring down rain, slowly raising the level of the water, and the hungry reptiles are determined to attack. You are on the last piece of high ground, but if you lower your guard, they will charge in and eat you. You are nearly exhausted, but you have a shovel and wield it as a weapon to ward off the aggressive alligators.

The thing is, you are standing right next to a drain valve. If you manage to turn the valve even slightly, it begins to open the drainpipes. If you turn it far enough, the drain will evacuate water faster than the rain is adding to it. The water level will fall, and the alligators will back off. Your task of keeping the alligators away would become less time-intensive, giving you more chances to open the valve even further. Your challenge is to force the alligators back far enough to buy the time to bend down and turn the valve.

That is the situation faced by many Stryker employees. The demands of keeping up with a relentless 20-percent increase could prove overwhelming. If you could get ahead of the demands just long enough to turn the valve and implement creative ideas and improvements, the floodgates would open and dramatically improve your daily situation.

The swamp had two effects on the creative spirit. One, people did not want to be surrounded by alligators and knew that beating them away with a shovel was not a long-term solution. We had to find some way to turn the valve. Two, scaring the alligators back would take considerable effort, and you would want to ensure that when you had the chance to turn the valve, you would be prepared with your best ideas so that no greasy hands or other basic oversight would cause your grip to slip. With enough determined attempts, you knew the swamp would drain.

A good example of the valve turning in action was a productivity-enhancing conversion driven by the purchasing and planning team on the production line of our medical–surgical bed in the mid-1990s. The bed was a highly customizable product, with hundreds or even thousands of potential configurations, depending on customer demands. Keeping inventory high enough to meet the configuration needs but low enough so as not to consume too much cash or warehouse space was a difficult challenge. The inventory requirements were initially set up using sophisticated Materials Requirements Planning (MRP) mainframe computer software that proved inadequate for the task. Parts shortages were common, and the assembly line experienced frequent shutdowns as a result. They were in the swamp, and the alligators were winning.

Conversion to a pull production system was how they would turn the valve. In a pull approach, simple visual cues managed by people doing the actual assembly would trigger the purchase of more parts. Essentially the supply would be pulled at the point of use. Such systems work most effectively when the triggers are fully integrated with the supplier's own planning systems and the cues can be sent directly to them. The creative buying and planning team believed they could devise a system that would work for their product line; but implementing the conversion would require considerable time setting up and coordinating the assembly line and the supply chain. To gain the time, they decided to overpurchase certain inventory for a brief period, expecting that it would reduce the considerable time spent expediting missing parts. They would gain the time by temporarily channeling the swamp water into a big bucket.

It worked. The parts converted to a pull system solidly reduced shortages on the assembly line. This allowed the buying and planning team more time to continue the conversions and convert more and more parts to the pull system. After about a year, nearly all parts were converted, and shortages declined dramatically. Even as the production requirements rose in the late 1990s and early 2000s, the team did not require additional buyers and planners. In fact, their core team became evangelists for the pull production approach, which proliferated throughout other teams in the plant.

It was an archetypical example of the swamp full of alligators: No one wanted to continue the shortage-prone MRP approach. The team devised a creative solution to the problem and unleashed further creativity in getting around the constraint of time to get the system implemented. Net inventory declined significantly, suppliers had a steadier flow of orders that improved their quality and costs, assembly seldom stopped, and the success became a model for other teams.

CAPITALIZING ON AVAILABLE CAPITAL

Other than the first year following the Howmedica acquisition, Stryker maintained an enviable balance sheet. No debt, loads of available cash, and strong retained earnings. With such a powerful financial position, you might guess that access to funding for new initiatives and going after new ideas was laissez-faire. It was not. Even with the prolific delegation of authority, focus through decentralization, individual autonomy, and accountability, all capital expenditure requests above a relatively small amount went through the corporate headquarters; John Brown personally reviewed and signed every single one. Again, this seeming constraint on a vital resource actually became a catalyst for unleashing creativity.

Corporate approval of capital projects leveled the playing field between divisions. Even in the dark days of Medical's initial debacle in the medical–surgical bed frontal assault, we were able to get access to capital for projects that showed a clear benefit toward 20-percent earnings growth. I submitted one of the largest requests for manufacturing machinery at a time when Medical, if left to its own means, would never have considered such a program. Corporate's tight grip on the purse strings for large capital expenditures in a strange way helped generate support from the divisional leadership teams for creative deployment of the capital. Setting up an us-versus-them mentality engaged competitive spirits that helped the divisional leadership get behind creative ideas.

Although every division had an annual capital budget, the constraints of time and headcount frequently stalled capital expenditures more often than approval did. As a result, divisions were seldom constrained by their capital budgets. The toughest criterion to meet was the stringent payback standard. The corporate office demanded a straightforward short-term cash payback for most capital expenditures (acquisitions and facility construction being two notable exceptions). This aggressive payback threshold meant that those requesting capital needed to concentrate on their best ideas for new machinery, equipment, tooling, and new product programs. It also meant that projects and programs that met the payback criteria were likely to be approved. Over the years, I sent millions of dollars in expenditure requests to corporate. Although some would generate considerable conversation and discussion, none were refused.

Obtaining the funding to complete tooling for our internationally focused M1 roll-in ambulance stretcher was probably the most challenging approval process. Since the majority of the profits would flow through the international divisions, they were required to agree to the expenditure and sign up for the sales. Thankfully, the leaders in Germany, Australia, and the United Kingdom recognized the potential of the product and agreed to the numbers. With agreement that the capital request would deliver the expected payback, the corporation approved M1. As a result, our global presence in EMS significantly expanded.

COUNTING ON HEADCOUNT

Of all the resources required for innovation, the most constrained was headcount. Innovators found time through a variety of means such as overordering to get ahead of their need. They found capital by going to the corporate bank and justifying its expenditure against the impact on 20-percent earnings growth. Headcount was an entirely different matter.

In a company doubling earnings every 3.7 years, headcount could very easily get out of control. Even if wage increases just kept pace with inflation, payroll could rise precipitously. Personnel additions did not require corporate approval like capital did; that would actually have removed some accountability from the divisions and would likely have led to far too many hires. Instead, Brown placed the responsibility directly on the divisional leaders. Those who grew headcount ahead of their sales and earnings would receive harsh criticism. If it appeared out of control, a division would find itself under a complete hiring freeze to be lifted only when earnings caught up with the burgeoning expansion of the ranks.

Again, the constraint stimulated some of the most significant innovations developed within the company. Each new opening was precious. Divisions could not afford to devote their valuable headcount adds to anything but the best talent. Finding people who would blossom in the demanding, purpose-focused atmosphere and embrace the obsession with growth was a challenging task. Managers who were hiring—and, most important, the divisional HR teams—became firmly resolved to optimize the effectiveness of the selection process.

Today, nearly every successful CEO touts similar ideas about the importance of talent. Senior managers in most Fortune 500 companies talk about the importance of surrounding themselves with the best people. We hear some form of *people are our number one asset* espoused by almost every corporate chieftain. In the late 1970s, 1980s, and early 1990s, such a philosophy was not nearly as widespread. Stryker was at the leading edge in adopting a talent-based approach.

Over three decades, unleashed creativity in the HR teams led to development of high-impact tools and techniques that turned the often mistake-prone, random crapshoot process of selecting new talent into a science.

The most significant advancements started in the early 1990s. As divisions experimented with techniques to improve their recruiting and interview methods, one division struck gold. Stryker Instruments discovered that using profiling tools developed by Gallup greatly helped define a prospective sales candidate's strengths and weaknesses. Statistically validated psychological assessments completed by Gallup's trained analysts during special candidate phone interviews provided increased accuracy in assessing the fit for Stryker's environment. Hiring salespeople whose strength profiles were congruent with those of other top sales performers dramatically improved recruiting results.

Instruments began to hire sales professionals who naturally flourished in the high-autonomy, straight-commission, you-eat-what-you-kill atmosphere. The division was at the tip of the spear in developing Stryker's relationship with Gallup and the talent-based offense that followed. Very soon their sister division Endoscopy began using the sales profiles and experiencing similar results.

For the rest of us, it was as if Gallup and the Surgical team had developed a new weapons technology that fundamentally altered the balance in combat, similar to how the first tanks broke the gridlock in World War I. Some were concerned about the invasive nature of the profiles and questioned whether they would make the grade if it had been a part of their own hiring process, but it was difficult to argue with the success. Surgical's sales teams were the focus of a 1994 *Sales and Marketing Management* magazine cover story, entitled "20 Percent—OR Else!"

Seeing considerable success in sales, Surgical quickly began applying the talent-based approach to engineers, accountants, buyer/planners, and other roles throughout the division. Again, the positive impact was almost immediate. Gallup's rigorous adherence to statistical principles dovetailed well with Stryker's results-based culture, and the Surgical leadership wholeheartedly embraced strengths-based hiring. As Gallup developed deeper relationships with Surgical's HR leaders, their influence spread. Seeking similar success, every division initiated and began expanding their work with Gallup by the end of the 1990s.

In his 2015 interview, Brown noted, "I would say that the best thing that happened to us in terms of recruiting was Gallup. I really give them a lot of credit for helping us evaluate people for their ability to fit in. As the years went on, Stryker developed a very unique personality as a company. Some used to say, 'Everybody wants a job at Stryker until they get one.' The demands were very high, and it took a unique personality to fit in. It took people who had a burning ambition to be successful. You saw that from people on the line to the salespeople to middle management to senior management."

Gallup gave us tools to identify candidates who possessed those unique personalities.

With its ranks exploding to well over 16,000 employees, finding such people year after year was a monumental task. The constraints on headcount served to unleash the creativity of the HR teams. Their partnership with Gallup introduced game-changing selection techniques that fundamentally improved the efficacy of our employee selection process. Starting with the Surgical sales teams, the approach proliferated through all the divisions and nearly every role in the company. The resulting increase in the number of people whose personal strengths were aligned with their roles in Stryker's aggressive goal-obsessed atmosphere was transformational.

24

CONTINUOUS

IMPROVEMENT

AT STRYKER

The drive for continuous improvement was a powerful force throughout Stryker. It was omnipresent in the product-development process and represented by a passionate quest deeply embedded in the ethos of the quality assurance, regulatory affairs, and manufacturing organizations. Advancements in the logistics and product delivery process, especially for implants, were also profound. Innovative methodologies to get the exact right implant into the surgeon's hands at the critical time were substantial contributions to what became far-reaching improvements in orthopedic implant procedures around the globe.

Nonetheless, there was one area that affected nearly everyone and that had a deep influence throughout the company. Inspired by the obsession to contribute to 20-percent growth, the divisional HR teams explored methods to improve management, leadership, and employee engagement in Stryker's ever-expanding workforce. Over time, the fruits of these efforts became force multipliers for almost every team within the organization and helped proliferate the 20-percent obsession as the company grew to over $1 billion in annual revenue.

As you know, Stryker's partnership with Gallup began with developing profiles and improving effectiveness with the recruiting and selection process. The momentous refinement of our ability to hire people whose fundamental strengths fit the organizational climate had far-reaching effects.

Looking back, John Brown noted, "Gallup really did have a unique approach, and I continue to give them a lot of credit for our success in helping us define the selection process, helping us make sure that we got the best talent."

To build on this success, the divisional HR teams and leaders sought creative techniques to further spread the 20-percent obsession and even more fully engage the hearts and minds of the steadily increasing talent in the employee base. Osteonics dove headlong into team-based manufacturing, eliminating layers of supervision on the factory floor, and in 1998, *Industry Week* recognized the plant in Allendale, New Jersey, as one of the ten best manufacturing plants in the nation.

The Surgical Group collaborated with Gallup to expand the success with selection to internal management and leadership. When Brown recombined the bed and stretcher divisions in the mid 1990s, he had asked me to investigate finding a partner, outside of Gallup, that would help Medical build its own unique methodology in driving engagement. However, as the battle with Hill-Rom became even bloodier, it was apparent that we did not have the time or resources to pursue this in full force. Brown began to ask Medical to adopt many of the tools being developed in the Surgical Group. With the acquisition of Howmedica in the late 1990s, he shifted that adoption into overdrive.

In previous chapters, I described the difficult entry of the Medical Division into the medical–surgical bed market. As we left that story, Medical had finally figured out how to attack a vulnerable flank of the monolithic competitor, Hill-Rom. Stryker had acquired Howmedica, and Brown moved Medical into a new grouping of divisions named the Medical–Surgical Group, led by the longtime Surgical president, Ron Elenbaas.

THE OFFENSE

By that time, the leadership and HR teams in Surgical's two founding divisions were deep into the evolution of what became known as *the Offense*—the aforementioned approach to recruiting conjoined with a powerful set of leadership and management tools and techniques that had been refined over many years. I was able to experience firsthand the powerful impact of rapidly implementing an evolved, continuous improvement effort. The effect was most immediate in sales, where despite the repositioning of the bed, results were still lagging.

As a part of the reorganization, Elenbaas decided to come in and lead Medical until he could find the right General Manager (GM). He moved his office into the Medical building and dug into the business. The effect was uplifting and immediate. Elenbaas was the type of charismatic leader who raises the energy in a room immediately. Given his exceptional history of performance, Elenbaas also had complete and unwavering support from John Brown to turn Medical around.

He assessed the situation for what it was: Medical had highly competitive products in nearly every segment in which it competed. With the Secure bed and its proprietary patient-safety technology, complemented by the best-in-class stretcher line, he saw the chance to do to Hill-Rom what the Surgical Instruments Division had done to its competitors in the 1990s.

The Secure bed was already attacking Hill-Rom at a vulnerable flank, and Elenbaas saw no issues with the basic strategy. It was a matter of execution, doing what Stryker did best with a needed emphasis on the third leg of the *invent it, make it, sell it* stool. It was time to implement the Offense.

With John Brown's support, Elenbaas reached out into the Stryker organization and brought one of his protégés from Europe to become Medical's GM. To address the exhausted sales team, the new GM brought in Jim Heath, a longtime Stryker Surgical veteran and former collegiate football coach who had led sales regions and Surgical's corporate accounts teams to great success. Heath came in deeply indoctrinated in the Offense and was unencumbered by the recent disastrous history in the bed market. It was fascinating to witness how his quick implementation of the Offense completely changed the game within Medical's dispirited sales team.

The hangover from ruinous frontal assaults against Hill-Rom had left a defeatist attitude and an underlying sense that Medical's behemoth enemy might be unbeatable. Nonetheless, Heath saw that across the country individual stars in the sales team were winning. These talented reps had taken beachheads in their territories and were forging a path with the Secure message, capitalizing on the many tools coming out of the marketing team.

In the microcosm of Medical's sales, the Offense essentially had five key tenets:

- Refining and committing to hiring profiles for the sales team
- Ensuring the right fit in management and support roles
- Strengths-based management and coaching
- A focus on individual and team engagement
- Stryker's climate of purpose-driven obsession

Having participated in the continuous improvement effort that developed these tenets within Surgical, Heath had a clear vision of the endgame and the necessary steps to get there. The implementation at Medical illustrates how powerful a continuous improvement effort becomes after years of fine-tuning.

HIRING PROFILES

The first step was to refine the selection profiles for Medical's sales team. By studying the most successful reps in conjunction with Gallup, they adjusted the definition of a candidate's congruency with the selection profile. The end result was a better, more tuned selection tool. Surgical had simplified Gallup's feedback criteria by assigning a letter grade to the congruency assessment. An A was congruent, a B was congruent with qualifications, and a C was incongruent. Eventually, the managers at Surgical took to hiring only candidates with an A or A+ on the assessment. When Heath took over, he made it official policy to only accept A-level salespeople.

VARSITY-LEVEL MANAGERS

For sales, as in most professions, the top individual contributors do not necessarily make the best managers. Many people aspire to management because their desire for achievement or a powerful ego forces them into it. Once they are faced with the day-to-day issues of managing people and the selfless aspects of working to make others successful, they long to return to the more easily defined battles of selling. Great managers care about their people. They get a kick out of building teams, helping people improve, and giving their subordinates a chance to do what they do best every day.

Ensuring the right fit for people managing or supporting Heath's sales team was the next challenge. Again, Surgical had worked over several years to develop screening profiles for sales managers. After years of justifying sales management selections to John Brown in monthly financial reviews, they had refined the process to a science, gaining his endorsement. Heath found that some folks were misplaced on the team and set about making appropriate changes.

STRENGTHS-BASED MANAGEMENT AND COACHING

The third crucial tenet was the idea of strengths-based management. It was not enough to simply hire people with the right profiles. Like Dibella, when deciding on the roles for each company in developing the playbook, or Brown throughout his history at Stryker, managing people by working to maximize their strengths and helping them deal with their weaknesses is essential. Leaders and managers require a realistic understanding of individual human strengths and weaknesses to do that.

The Offense put additional science behind this philosophy. It served to institutionalize what came naturally to leaders like Dibella and Brown. Since the mid-1990s, Stryker's divisional leaders had been attending Gallup's Leadership Academy. Most attendees, myself included, would say that Gallup's course was among the most influential development experiences of their professional life. Gallup provided a comprehensive vocabulary and defined methodology around what John Brown had been doing for years.

Professional development courses and the proliferation of management tools and aids became a source of constant improvement. Heath sent Medical's sales managers and highly influential salespeople to Gallup courses. Those under his leadership were expected to immediately capitalize on and use their learning. It was all part of expanding the managers' knowledge of human strengths.

To best appreciate their people's strengths and weaknesses, managers initially relied on the hiring profiles, along with their gut assessments and experiences with each individual salesperson. However, the profiles were meant to screen candidates and were specific to a position; they were not necessarily broad definitions of a person's inherent strengths outside of that specific role. The understanding of strengths improved significantly with Gallup's later development of the Clifton StrengthsFinder. It all provided a common language about personal strengths and weakness. Like Adam in the Garden of Eden, having a name for things brought greater meaning and awareness. Incorporating the profile themes and then StrengthsFinder into the management approach helped take the Offense to even higher levels.

As more people were trained and educated about this new terminology, the ability to attach clear vocabulary to individual traits facilitated conversations that had often been clumsy and prone to misunderstanding before. It greatly assisted managers in coaching their people.

For example, the tendency to automatically turn thoughts into action now had a name: A person who does this is called an *activator*. Someone with the ability to figure out how all the pieces can be organized for maximum productivity is an *arranger*. An employee with the innate desire to see something good and work to make it great could be summed up in one word: This person is a *maximizer*. Gallup identified thirty-four different themes that became part of the everyday language at Stryker.

INDIVIDUAL AND TEAM ENGAGEMENT

Focusing on employee engagement was the next significant element of the Offense. It was about empowering the obsession. Here, again, the partnership with Gallup provided a valuable tool. After exhaustive study and analysis of the effectiveness of small workgroups in many different settings and companies, including Stryker, Gallup uncovered a strong statistical correlation between the answers people gave to twelve specific questions on an anonymous survey and the effectiveness or cohesion of the workgroup. They branded this the *Q12* survey, and Stryker became one of its staunchest proponents. The Surgical Group in particular developed a comprehensive method of facilitated team discussions around the survey results, with open conversation and specific follow-up actions agreed on by the managers. Heath brought the whole approach to the sales team.

Gallup's researchers also found that a person's first-line supervisor had the greatest impact on the Q12 answers. Dovetailing on the already pervasive delegation of authority in the company, the Offense doubled down on the criticality of the first-line supervisor. Individual managers and HR team members developed many additional tools and techniques to assist folks in addressing their team's Q12 feedback. Heath brought knowledge of many of the best practices from the Surgical Group. Over his tenure in Medical sales, the team went from having one of the lowest composite Q12 scores in the company to having one of the highest.

THE ESSENTIAL ELEMENTS: 20 PERCENT

The final critical elements of the Offense were supercharging the existing foundations of the Stryker approach to sales that we covered in previous sections. Heath and the new GM ensured that Medical absolutely aligned the division to support the sales team. Performance for salespeople and managers was vigorously racked and stacked. Every rep had a chart reviewed every month. The absolute clarity of 20 percent and an obsession with achieving it infused the team. The Offense was incomplete without all the Stryker fundamentals.

The end result of these efforts was a phenomenal turnaround in the sales momentum for Medical's hospital-focused sales team. The medical–surgical bed and every other hospital product benefited. John Brown's perseverance through the trials of the Medical division during the late 1990s paid great benefits. Medical went from the laggard of the company to the best-performing division over the next decade. The impact of a nearly decade-long continuous improvement effort all being implemented at the same time completely changed the face of Medical's hospital-focused sales team.

A CAPTAIN OF INDUSTRY

Since the industrial revolution, the great captains of industry have been a source of intense curiosity for us. We see in them an uncanny ability to push the human race forward. We study them and dissect their careers, attempting to identify the unique traits that led to their success. When we think ingenuity, Edison and Jobs come to mind. Mass production elicits Ford. Unbounded ambition conjures Rockefeller. Relentlessness drive gives us Gates. Deal-making savvy leads to J. P. Morgan. We see in all of them a rare combination of ambition, creativity, focus, and capability. What is often missing from the history books is that these leaders also had an extraordinary ability to capture the hearts of the people in their companies and inspire them to phenomenal heights. They set a clear and simple purpose for their organization. They gathered around them a dedicated group as obsessed with achieving that purpose as they were. And they allowed the collective creativity of everyone on the team to shine.

John Brown never sought fame or notoriety. His most notable life's work was building a small business that someone else had started into the most respected firm of its kind in the world. The notoriety he has received came as a result of the extraordinary accomplishments of that business and the curiosity others have had seeking to understand how he inspired such exceptional results. The anomaly of twenty-eight consecutive years of 20-percent growth seems almost supernatural. But he built Stryker in a fashion similar to how the great captains built their companies.

Each in their unique way, these remarkable leaders got into the minds of their subordinates. Brown did so by establishing a clear and unequivocal goal; by setting the quintessential example of a work ethic; by developing an empowering, decentralized atmosphere with every incentive aligned with the goal; and by unleashing the creativity of thousands through the focusing lens of that unique structure. Working at Stryker changed people; and in the process, they changed the company and produced inventions that have improved lives all over the world. In attempting to explain how all that happened, I am left with the conclusion that in some enigmatic fashion, leaders such as John Brown touch people's souls.

Conclusion

THE REMARKABLE

INFLUENCE OF

EXTRAORDINARY LEADERS

Every once in a while an individual accomplishes something truly remarkable. Perhaps because the achievement is unexpected and far beyond what we thought possible, the entire world takes notice. Names like Michael Jordan, Serena Williams, Usain Bolt, Pelé, Bobby Fischer, Tom Brady, Michael Phelps, and Simone Biles bring images of excellence to mind for most of us. We study these people, hoping to understand what is different about them. We seek to emulate what they did in training, how they approached their game, and the new techniques they unleashed on the world.

Perhaps even more, we admire teams or organizations that radically alter the landscape for a large portion of humanity. In many cases, the extraordinary capability of these teams alters the course of history.

The phalanx of Alexander the Great and Caesar's Roman legions are two military examples. Business history would not be the same without notable game-altering organizations, including the Carnegie Steel Company, John D. Rockefeller's Standard Oil Company, the Edison Electric Light Company (now GE), the Walt Disney Corporation, and Steve Jobs's Apple. In each instance, a team of driven human beings led by an extraordinary leader accomplished the incredible and delivered products that changed the world.

These are companies and military organizations that altered the global landscape in a visible and widely recognized fashion. There is a great deal written about what they did and how they did it. However, those seeking insights into the secrets of success from the fabled experiences are often disappointed. Fame has a way of clouding the essential elements or obscuring the facts. Pundits overanalyze, and the media embellishes, overlooking facts that may not attract as much interest or advance the ideological leanings of the media outlet. A recent illustration of this is the near-complete election-day surprise at the outcome of 2016's US presidential election. Few news services accurately understood the support Trump was getting from actual voters in key electoral college states; even fewer made it part of their reports.

Removed from the limelight, the experience of lesser-known leaders and organizations may be, in many ways, purer sources of learning. Their history is unadorned by media spin. Understanding the inner workings that allowed less-celebrated organizations to achieve extraordinary results in more obscure fields can reveal secrets missed or distorted by the sheer volume of research in the more common examples. These are uncomplicated secrets all of us can use to bring about exceptional results for our teams or businesses. Their leaders may not capture the fame of Steve Jobs, but their impact within their close-knit organizations could be just as significant or even more so.

Throughout this book, I have endeavored to present such an insider's view of two exceptional organizations and the remarkable influence of their extraordinary leaders. I was lucky enough to be a part of combined arms Task Force 4-68 in the US Army and international medical-device corporation Stryker while they each achieved what most believed was impossible. Although not everything was perfect, the sheer statistical anomaly of the achievements made for two stories that deserved to be told. These organizations and their leaders did something incredibly unique. My hope has been that an insider's perspective has helped you uncover meaningful insights and new concepts. What surfaces in these lesser-known stories are the simple truths of the deep and pervasive impact the top leader had in totally engaging hearts and minds throughout their organizations. This was the magic that drove extraordinary results.

Certainly the focus of these two organizations was very different. Despite that, the powerful emotional ties and deep sense of commitment that insiders experienced in each organization was remarkably similar. At the top was a leader whose influence on the hearts and minds of nearly every member of the team was profound and unmistakable. They created distinct, high-achieving, nearly fanatical cultures.

Each delivered extraordinary results, but this was never intended as a book about how to replicate these two leaders. They were very different people, and they led with somewhat contrasting styles. My primary intent was to focus on the influence these two markedly dissimilar leaders wielded throughout their organizations. If anything about their stories can be duplicated, it is the clarity, obsession, and unleashing of ingenuity. That is what drove the very similar collective consciousness out of which exceptional results were a seemingly inevitable outcome. These are special lessons about inspiring human organizations.

Although I am analytical by nature and enjoy theses that are backed by exhaustive statistics and research, what I have told regarding these two organizations are their stories. Unlike an academic work about something researched from a distance, this was about direct observations and revelations from someone lucky enough to have lived through two amazing experiences. Witnessing a great leader build a high-performance organization is an emotional event. Understanding the passions, concerns, and psychology experienced by members of the unit or business as events unfolded tells a story that can go beyond the statistics. There is much to be learned from these great leaders, and I hope you found these stories and explanations full of insights that you can use at whatever level you work in your organization. If you can recognize those patterns as they occur—or do not occur—in your own organization, there is a chance to help steer events and collective will toward excellence.

As a final comment, I also had the opportunity to stay with these organizations following the departure or retirement of their outstanding leaders. Although this was heart-wrenching to experience, these transitions presented valuable insights as the organizations transformed from great to average. 4-68 Armor maintained some of its winning ways following Dibella's change of command; but the new commander was out to make his mark and build his own team, and no unit has ever won every battle at NTC since. Stryker is still a very good company, highly admired in the medical-device industry, but the days of consistent 20-percent earnings growth are a distant memory. The organizations did not fall into the abyss; they just became normal.

Having lived through it twice, the most distressing part of the process is that depressing feeling that occurs when the energy and directed esprit dissipates. Without the absolute clarity of a single purpose, the obsession fades, and creative activities lose focus. This does not happen in an instant but in a collection of moments over an extended period. These great organizations surrendered to become merely good in the same way they were built to be extraordinary—one brick at a time. Nonetheless, the experiences left me convinced that such decline is not inevitable. I am optimistic that providing insights may help prevent this decay in organizations that are currently operating at high levels. Perhaps that will be the subject of a future work.

ACKNOWLEDGMENTS

Writing this work has been a labor of love. I am eternally grateful for the incredible experiences I had in these two organizations. It was heartwarming to listen to the recollections of so many others who were equally touched. In every instance it took little but an inquiry to have a thoughtful conversation with others who lived through it. For some it had been many years since their time at Stryker, or up to thirty years after that fabled NTC rotation—yet they still remembered everything as if it happened yesterday.

I am, of course, deeply indebted to Fred and John for their leadership, their mentorship, and their friendship. To have the opportunity to work under one such extraordinary leader would have been the event of a lifetime. Working under two was simply miraculous. The experiences made me a better leader, a better mentor, and a better person.

I would like to thank all the soldiers from Task Force 4-68 and our higher leadership. We lived through a peacetime experience that approached, in a small way, the bonding events that happen in a war. I am particularly grateful to those who connected after so many years: Joe Moore, for his excellent recollection of the NTC engagements; Dave

Styles, Mark Pires, and Tommy Piskel for their advice and insights; and fellow platoon leader Bobby Campbell for his engaging recollection of the 4-68 experience.

There are so many to acknowledge over my twenty-three years at Stryker that I can't begin to do you all justice. Throughout my career I had the chance to lead and be a part of some absolutely fabulous teams of truly exceptional people. In reflecting on this book, let me single out just a few: Harry Carmitchel for taking a chance and hiring a tank officer to take the reins of his division's most important project; for their insightful thoughts and recollections: Matt Alves, Dean Bergy, Phil Brule, Mark Fletcher, Jim Heath, Ken Palmer, and John Saunders.

Karl Ostroski gave me the lead to *New York Times* best-selling author Paul Spiegelman, with whom the rejection-ridden process of finding an agent started to come to a close. Can't thank these two enough. I'm deeply indebted to the team at Greenleaf for their courage in taking a chance on this first-time author: Justin Branch for seeing the potential; Nathan True for edits and changes that made the work truly come together; and Tyler LeBleu and his production team for their diligence.

The development of this manuscript has been a family affair. Many thanks for the constant and loving support of my incredible wife, Gail. For help with edits and ideas on the first clumsy drafts: Ryan Umberger; Dan Straface; and my father, Dave Morton. Finally, to all my daughters, who sometimes wondered where Dad was and what he was doing on all those late nights and travels, perhaps now you will understand a little more how lucky we were to benefit from my being a part of these two awesome organizations.

Appendix A

ARMY ORGANIZATIONAL STRUCTURE

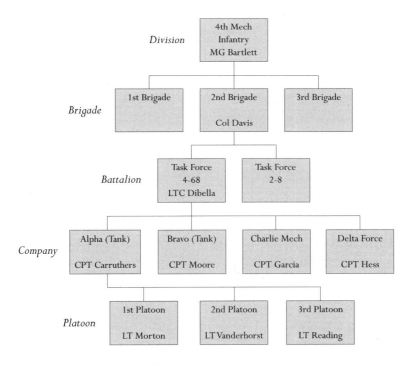

Appendix B

STRYKER ORGANIZATIONAL STRUCTURE

CIRCA 1990s

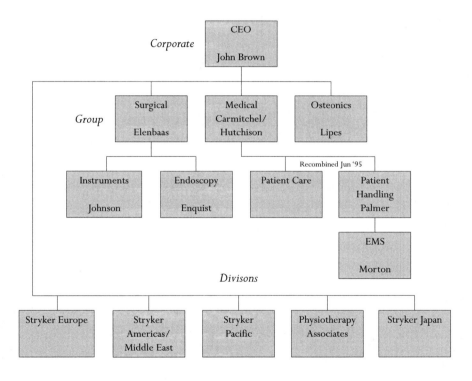

ABOUT THE AUTHOR

West Point distinguished graduate Gary Morton had a five-year career as a tank officer, the highlight of which was being part of an extraordinary unit that achieved unprecedented results at the US Army's grueling National Training Center—the only unit to ever win every simulated battle it fought. Gary also graduated with an MS degree from the University of Southern California with honors. After the Army, he joined medical-device manufacturer Stryker, where he held positions of increasing responsibility in project management, engineering, R&D, operations, marketing, and business leadership, all culminating in twelve years as Vice President and General Manager of the EMS equipment business that he cofounded. An innovative juggernaut, Stryker EMS grew to become the global leader in patient-handling equipment for the ambulance market. His team introduced game-changing products that have redefined how paramedics handle patients in emergency situations throughout the developed world. Today, he is retired from Stryker and lives with his wife in the Midwest, where he writes and invests. You can learn more at www.iGaryMorton.com.

A FINAL REQUEST

I f this book impacted you in a positive way, please recommend it. Keeping with the flow of the three magical metathemes capturing the essence of these leaders' influence, you can make a difference by motivating at least three other people to pick up and read about these extraordinary leaders. Over time, this "power of three" will spread the ideas presented in these pages, and the thousands of hours spent creating this work will have lasting impact.

Most books by first-time authors sell fewer than than 1,000 copies; then again, most units get thrashed by the OPFOR at NTC or never even dream of twenty-eight years of 20-percent growth. Every positive review on Amazon, iBooks, Barnes&Noble, or other media outlets will spread the leadership lessons. Rate the book or write a short review. Be aware that a 4.5 out of 5 is the average score for an influential work of this type, and consider giving it a five. Leaders John Brown and Fred Dibella redefined the scale of organizational success, and you can be a part of that legacy by spreading the stories of their achievements.

Thank You,
Gary T. Morton